Gardens of Intelligence

Designing Robust Digital Market and Competitive Intelligence Platforms

Gabriel Anderbjörk

Jesper E. Martell

Technics Publications

TECHNICS PUBLICATIONS
TECHNOLOGY / LEADERSHIP

115 Linda Vista
Sedona, AZ 86336 USA
https://www.TechnicsPub.com

Edited by Kerri Marikakis
Cover design by Lorena Molinari
Illustrations by Torbjörn Johansson

First Printing 2021

ISBN, print ed. 9781634629331
ISBN, Kindle ed. 9781634629348
ISBN, ePub ed. 9781634629355
ISBN, PDF ed. 9781634629362

Library of Congress Control Number: 2021939479

Praise

"I have known the authors since they were changing Ericsson CI from within, pioneering the global intelligence network and using it to affect innumerous decisions throughout the company. Their practical perspective is unparalleled in the field on how CI affects the bottom line. Together they have more experience with platforms in more companies than all of us combined and the beauty of their approach is that they chart a path to getting many different people at the organization to look at a stream of info and say, *hold on*. Have you thought of…? So, what are the six steps to their "Garden of Intelligence"? Oh, for God sakes I am not going to describe it. Just read it!"

Benjamin Gilad

Co-founder of the Academy of Competitive Intelligence

"Regardless of whether you are starting out or a seasoned market and competitive insight professional you have to read this. Not only does it provide a perspective from two gentlemen who have been at the coal face of practicing market and competitive intelligence at Ericsson at its height but have used and understood those well-trodden frameworks and approaches and digitized them. The book does a fantastic job to provide a balanced view around the when and how to bring in technology to go beyond the collection phase of creating the knowledge and the foreknowledge of the market around you as a prelude to decision making and action. This is complemented by case studies of businesses Jesper and Gabriel have worked with to advance their businesses' insight capabilities as competitive advantages. A great title to address the velocity of change powered by the Internet to reduce time to insight."

Andrew Beurschgens

Head, Market and Competitive Intelligence, BT

"I recommend this book to my customers, so they make an impact on the bottom line; to my students so that they can have an impact on the professional world; and just about anyone interested in actually making an impact. This is the power of Garden of Intelligence!"

Luis Madureira

Managing Partner @ UBERBRANDS, CIP-II, CI Fellow

Contents

About the Authors

Gabriel Anderbjörk and Jesper Martell have collaborated since 1994 when they met at Ericsson, a telecommunications company in Stockholm, Sweden, as the core of the corporate competitive intelligence team. In January 1999, they teamed up with a third colleague to found the software company Comintelli (www.comintelli.com). Comintelli believes that *information* is one of the most valuable assets possessed by an organization and should be managed as such.

Comintelli was a market pioneer for automation in information classification and dissemination. At the time, it was almost unheard of to mix external information with internal content in the same classification structures and user interfaces. Furthermore, the focus on context-driven information models and algorithms (taxonomies), rather than prevailing content-driven structures, changed how many customers approached the entire field of information management.

Since then, the authors have engaged with and helped hundreds of organizations, multinational companies, and governmental organizations in most corners of the world to develop and implement intelligence operations and knowledge management platforms. Their joint experience of more than 50 years in the Market and Competitive Intelligence (MCI) field is simply unrivaled.

Gabriel Anderbjörk is a true innovator and entrepreneur within the fields of Information Management, Knowledge Management, and Enterprise Intelligence. The latter sprung a deep interest in and insight into varied global business cultures and their impact on international Competitive Intelligence (CI) operations. His professional experience spans more than 25 years and includes major projects worldwide.

Today, Gabriel is the founder and Chief Executive Officer (CEO) of Inzyon (www.inzyon.com), an organization that develops and delivers advanced insights management environments. Previously, he was the Director of Competitive Intelligence at the telecom company Ericsson, co-founder of Comintelli, and worked as a structured trade finance analyst at Citigroup European HQ.

Since leaving Ericsson, Gabriel has enjoyed providing advisory and consulting services to numerous management teams within regional and global companies such as AstraZeneca, Bayer, BBC, Fortum, Interpol, Olympus, Roche, Skanska, Volvo Cars, and Yokogawa. He has also served as a senior advisor on information modeling and process development in select European governmental organizations.

Gabriel frequently speaks on his topics of expertise and participates in international panels. He has lectured at the top European business schools INSEAD and Stockholm School of Economics, presented at international webinars, and contributed to Romanian national TV business news. Furthermore, he has led courses for several Stockholm University international executive business training programs. Gabriel's publications include articles in the SCIP *Competitive Intelligence Magazine* and published papers on information theory. Parallel to his work at Inzyon, he also manages his own think tank company, Intheo (www.intheo.se), further developing his theories on Information-Centric Management.

Gabriel holds a BA degree in physics from Lund University, Sweden, and an MBA from London Business School.

Jesper Ejdling Martell is a highly experienced CI professional, having worked in the field since 1996—initially as a practitioner at telecom company Ericsson and later as a solution provider at Comintelli.

Today, he is the co-founder and Chief Executive Officer (CEO) of Comintelli (www.comintelli.com), a leading provider of award-winning competitive intelligence platform Intelligence2day® (www.intelligence2day.com).

Over the years, Jesper has served as a trusted advisor in CI-related matters for multinational companies and organizations, including AkzoNobel, Bayer, Dow AgroSciences, Ericsson, Essity, ExxonMobil, Interpol, Monsanto, Schott, Telia, and Tetra Pak.

Jesper has engaged in numerous presentations, courses, and webinars, sharing his Competitive Intelligence expertise with associations such as Strategic Competitive Intelligence Professionals (SCIP), Knowledge Management (KM) World, and Special Libraries Association (SLA). He also chaired CiMi.CON in Berlin, Europe's premier CI conference.

From 2013-2016, Jesper was a leading participant and sponsor of a 3-year research project at Södertörn University in Stockholm to study how the competitive intelligence (CI) and business analytics (BA) industries can meet challenges and utilize possibilities with social computing. The project, *Competitive Intelligence and Business Analytics: Social Computing for the Knowledge-Intensive Enterprise (CIBAS)*, was co-funded by the research financier, The Knowledge Foundation.

In 2016, SCIP (www.scip.org) named Jesper a Distinguished Member, recognizing his international achievement in the field for his unique contributions to the profession of intellectual advancement of intelligence and dedication to the SCIP Association and community of creators. Jesper currently chairs the SCIP Nordic chapter.

In 2020, Jesper was inducted into the Council of Competitive Intelligence Fellows (www.cifellows.com), recognizing his long-standing contributions to the CI profession. CI Fellows sustain and foster the CI discipline with roles as Ambassadors, Champions, Mentors, and Educators.

Jesper holds a Masters of Business Administration (MBA) from the Stockholm School of Economics.

The Stupidity of Artificial Intelligence

Is AI stupid?

I never actually understood the purpose of a foreword. I have read books where the foreword was longer than the book. Won't happen here. Who cares what I have to say? This is Gabriel's and Jesper's book based on their truly global track record.

I have known the authors since they were changing Ericsson from within, one CI bit at a time. Three guys in a huge conservative company, pioneering the global intelligence network, and using it to affect innumerous decisions throughout the company, from supply chain to strategic initiatives. That experience has given them practical perspective unparalleled in the field on how CI affects the bottom line. And I believe they have only wised up since then.

A little detour:

I love Ericsson. Under Gabriel and Jesper, it produced one of the world's most sophisticated CI programs way earlier than most other companies (surely way earlier than other Telcom.) I remember the first time I worked with it, eons ago. I was whisked to a winter retreat from hell in Lapland in February. I spent a week training a group of cadets in a program called BIAP- Business Intelligence Analysts Program (I think). I had two most memorable moments there, in the freezer: Looking out the window of my room I saw a group of naked men and women running in the snow. I decided I was hallucinating again. I wasn't. Swedes are like that. They make frozen lemonade out of frozen tundra. The second moment came in a war game mockup workshop where the young trainees, smart as a whip, briefed by Gabriel and his team, foresaw the future, long before management saw it. It's what CI is all about, isn't it?

Gabriel and Jesper left Ericsson long ago and started up new companies. Competitive intelligence wizards can do that since the profession is all about seeing the early signs of an evolving future. Entrepreneurship at its best. Out came Knowledge Xchanger and then Intelligence2day products, two pioneering CI platforms. And now there is Inzyon, an insight management platform. And these, as well as this book, address the core issue of getting MCI into the right hands at the right time.

The authors say, "MCI is the process of enhancing marketplace competitiveness through a greater understanding of a firm's competitive environment." I love this concise definition. But add AI/Machine Learning to the mix, and we get stupid. Why?

AI itself isn't stupid. It's just a program based on an algorithm, which is built on a model. But novices think AI will give them intelligence. It never will. It will help enormously in sifting through unimaginable amount of noise, and at the end, with machine learning and predictive analytics, it will fit the results better and better to our revealed (implicit) or declared (explicit) preferences. But it can't produce insight, only humans can. Moreover- it can't change preferences on its own, only the users can. As Groucho Marx, the greatest of all philosophers said, "Those are my principles, and if you don't like them... well, I have others." AI does that. You don't like that Netflix movie? It will recommend others; It does what we tell it to do until we change what we tell it we like.

Alas, we, collectively, as human managers and executives, are typically stupid when it comes to looking at what is not in front of our noses. That's where the MCI analyst comes in. Armed with a platform and AI/ML for searching the Milky Way galaxy, he or she are supposed to say: Hold on for a second. Have you thought of....?

The beauty of Gabriel's and Jesper's approach is that they chart a path to getting many different people at the organization to look at a stream of info and say, hold on. Have you thought of...? That is the 1-2% that is not obvious.

In this light, a platform may change the way management fundamentally look at MCI. Put it differently: In this day and age where "digitalization" is the magic wand, their platform-based process is just what may tilt the scale in favor of management taking it seriously as a game changer in the real competition for oh so scarce insights.

So, what are the six steps to their "Garden of Intelligence"? Oh, for god sakes I am not going to describe it. Just read it. The authors have more experience with platforms in more companies than all of us combined. Pay attention to the Carrier Wave and the 1-2% differential advantage which will keep your company competitive, while others are waiting for AI to magically produce competitiveness.

By Benjamin Gilad

Benjamin Gilad is a pioneer in the field of competitive Intelligence. He has published multiple books and articles on the subject, is a co-founder of the Academy of Competitive Intelligence and serves as a consultant for many Fortune 500 companies. He lives in Boca Raton, FL, US of A. He is not AI augmented.

What's in it for you?

Already working as Market and Competitive Intelligence (MCI) practitioners in the late 90s, we were struck by the lack of focus and structure in the MCI work of many organizations we encountered. Within our own industry, the pace of change was at that time probably the fastest of all, given international market deregulation for cellular networks and the race to claim de facto monopolies for specific technologies. At Ericsson, we built our own internal MCI platform, training program, and global analysis network that eventually, and measurably, contributed to group bottom-line results. CI legend Ben Gilad was our first true mentor and inspiration, and we were thrilled he accepted to write the foreword to this book.

We launched Comintelli in 1999, inspired by encouragement from companies who would later become some of our first customers. Since then, our customers and peers frequently ask for recommendations on MCI operations literature. We always respond by naming traditional books that focus more on analytics and less on processes and support systems.

For many years, we considered writing that sought-after book ourselves, with the lack of time as a barrier—until now. This book serves as the practical hands-on guidebook we wished we had while building a global MCI operation many years ago. Granted, it now includes some additional insights that probably didn't even exist at the time!

We hope you will enjoy reading it as much as we have enjoyed performing the relevant research over the last 20+ years and now, finally writing it!

Jack Welsh, the CEO of GE, once famously said that *"When the rate of change outside exceeds the rate of change inside, the end is in sight."* This has never been truer. Even though the concept of intelligence is far from new, its application must be updated to suit a more turbulent, evolving world.

Market and Competitive Intelligence directly impacts the ability to keep many parts of an organization healthy, strong, and competitive. This book, therefore, aims to target both:

- **Executives and decision-makers, or the *consumers* of intelligence.** Those who use it to understand their business landscape and anticipate future opportunities and threats.

- **Intelligence analysts/practitioners, or the *producers* of intelligence**. Those who were assigned the important task to track information and discover actionable insights.

With this book, we aim to bring intelligence into the future and the future into intelligence.

Enterprises realize they must prepare for varied business disruptions and change while transitioning to a digital economy. A prioritized agenda item for CEOs during this shift is to transform their corporations into more intelligent organizations. During uncertain times, real-time information from internal and external sources, combined with organizational learning and knowledge, enables enterprises to rapidly adjust and adapt.

This book explains how intelligence tools and technology are vital to transform into a digital business, as well as illustrate how investing in technology will provide the decision support required to create competitive advantages. Unlike many others on the topic, this book does *not* focus on analysis models, research tips, or future forecasts. Rather, this is a pragmatic, hands-on guide to help initiate, develop, implement and maintain MCI operations and platforms in organizations and enterprises.

The framework and ideas presented in the book are based both on our own practical experience in the last 25 years and research drawn from over 100 Competitive

Intelligence cases. These organizations range from large Fortune 500 companies to smaller analyst firms. They represent a variety of industries across many countries, as illustrated below. From this material, we have isolated common traits and characteristics of successful MCI platforms. These organizations are all truly at the forefront of Market and Competitive Intelligence.

AkzoNobel	Ericsson	Olympus
Amadeus	Essity	Owens Corning
Bayer	ExxonMobil	Roche
Biogen	GEA	SCA
Bristol Myers Squibb	Honeywell	Schott
British Telecom	HPE	Siemens
Corteva	Interpol	Telia
DOW AgroSciences	LexisNexis	Tetra Pak
Royal DSM	Medtronic	VodafoneZiggo
EnerSys	Monsanto	Volvo
	Nokia	Yokogawa

This book consists of four parts:

- **Part I—A Wild Grown Landscape.** The first part of the book (chapter 1 and 2) describes that the world has changed and **why** Market & Competitive Intelligence should be used to create insights that make your organization more future proof.

- **Part II—Growing a Garden.** The second part is the key part of the book (chapter 3 and 4). We describe **what** the Garden of Intelligence is – a management concept for developing successful Market & Competitive Intelligence capabilities. The framework is a step-by-step stairway to a blooming Garden of Intelligence that will reduce your time to insights and decisions.

- **PART III—Digging Deeper**. The third part provides more in-depth guidance into **how** to work with some key capability components that are essential for the buildup of Market & Competitive Intelligence, namely Information, Technology and People. Chapters 5 and 6 are about Information, chapters 7 and 8 covers Technology and chapters 9 and 10 deal with the People capability.

- **PART IV—Beyond the Garden Walls.** The final, fourth, part answers the "**Now what?**" question, i.e. what do you do with all your insights? Anyone who has attempted to develop a beautiful and long-lasting garden know that you

cannot relax just because your first rhododendrons are blooming and you have harvested your first sweet oranges. A garden needs constant attention and influences from the outside will be critical. Chapter 11 to 13 are there to provide a future perspective and inspiration.

We recommend you first skim through the book in full, just to acquaint yourself with its content. Then, engage in a self-assessment based on the framework outlined in Chapter 4—which level corresponds with your position? Continue to use this book as inspiration and guidance to eventually achieve a state-of-the-art MCI platform within your organization.

PART I

A Wild Grown Landscape

The first part of the book (Chapters 1 and 2) describe that the world has changed and **why** Market & Competitive Intelligence should be used to create insights that make your organization more future proof.

CHAPTER 1

Introducing Market and Competitive Intelligence (MCI)

Key MCI drivers

Let's start with a fundamental question: "Why do you need MCI?" This may sound like a tricky query to begin with, but the answer is simple: two major, parallel developments have created an unprecedented demand for MCI:

1. The pace of change is accelerating.
2. Big data creates information overload.

In the words of Jeff Bezos, founder and current CEO of Amazon, "In today's era of volatility, there is no other way but to re-invent. The only sustainable advantage you can have over others is agility, that's it. Because nothing else is sustainable, everything else you create, somebody else will replicate."

The world is changing. Competition is fierce. Market and Competitive Intelligence is more relevant than ever to generate insights that will successfully lead your organization into the future!

The pace of change is accelerating

Today, we live in a world marked by volatility, uncertainty, complexity, and ambiguity, otherwise known as a "VUCA" world. This is a world where Black Swans occur more frequently against the backdrop of business-as-usual crisis management; where companies are unable to predict outcomes both within and outside their home market or industry; where cause and effect form a complex web that makes it difficult to identify the root causes and problems faced by management; and where event significance is impossible to quantify. Since 2000, 52% of Fortune 500 companies have either faced bankruptcy, corporate takeover, or dissolution, illustrating the pace of change within the corporate arena. Smaller and mid-sized companies encounter this phenomenon at an even higher rate.

In this VUCA world, one must make quick decisions while still considering all relevant information. Leaders must create a sense of urgency and ensure all organization members understand the need for change.

To do this, organizations must ensure their employees can access the right information at the right time. Business productivity must also improve through internal collaboration and information-sharing practices.

Creating customized environments that foster flexible interaction and rapid adaptation to this optimized communication is truly the key to success.

Big data creates information overload

Overall, businesses are in a state of information overload, and the massive growth of unstructured knowledge makes it difficult to access relevant and accurate information. Content is often stored in unique silos that are rarely shared, making it difficult to know which data is already there for the taking.

The challenge is not finding information. The challenge is discovering golden signals amongst all the noise.

However, it's important to note that this information jungle also provides enormous opportunities for those with the tools and solutions available to explore it. The question is: How can organizations enable access to useful information for their employees?

Possessing vast amounts of data is of little value in and of itself, especially when it resides in silos—both internally across various departments and externally across various sources and social media channels. What increasingly separates the winners from the losers is transforming data into insights about consumer motivations and then transforming that acumen into strategy.

Decision-making requires intelligence

All of this complexity, change, and information overload complicates the life of a decision-maker. Each additional piece of information you receive makes it more difficult to digest the material and distinguish important/unimportant factors when making decisions. The fear of missing an important piece of the puzzle continues to grow and can lead to "decision paralysis," wherein flawed, or even worse, *no* decisions are made.

The fear of missing an important piece of the puzzle continues to grow and can lead to "decision paralysis."

Most decision-makers don't have the time, nor the skills, to process and filter all relevant information. This is where Market and Competitive Intelligence professionals step in to support decision-makers by drawing conclusions and providing insights.

With the decision support provided by MCI, organizations are equipped with an enhanced map of their business environment so they can discern which way to go, how to compete, and ultimately grow and succeed as an organization.

The business impact of MCI

MCI is about systematically gathering, analyzing, and managing information about your business landscape. It helps drive decisions that improve your competitive advantage. Ultimately, it is the process of enhancing and fortifying your position by leveraging an improved map of your business environment.

MCI is about systematically gathering, analyzing, and managing information about your business landscape. It helps drive decisions that improve your competitive advantage.

All companies strive (or should strive) to serve as the provider of choice for all prospective and current customers of their products or services. The only requirement to succeed (according to available management literature), is to deploy a strategy that ensures an optimal competitive position for an organization's products or services within a target market(s). Easier said than done? Yes, of course, yet it remains the ultimate goal, and companies dedicate significant resources in their quest to achieve this.

Can MCI help? Yes, big time! And we are willing to spout the provocative argument that companies without MCI will fall behind, as competitors that *do* employ these strategies will continuously outperform their peers. Lacking adequate MCI capabilities leads to consequences that fall into two categories, generally speaking: missed business opportunities and exposure to unforeseen threats.

Fundamentally, organizations implement MCI to improve decision-making in market positioning and strategic competitiveness: aligning corporate strategy, tactics, and communication with market expectations, regulations, and competition. With certainty, we can say that a gap will always exist between an organization's position and ideal footing within the market, and MCI's task is to constantly strive to minimize such disparities. If truly successful, this is reduced to a level that sees the organization as the industry leader with the smallest possible market gap and subsequent ability to attract the most customers.

MCI capabilities

MCI and its intelligence synonyms share one thing in common: the massive quantity of information and people-to-people communication that must be managed. MCI must therefore understand the market and related criteria at an extraordinary level and the organization's current positioning and capabilities. This requires significant information and analytics resources alongside a well-developed subject matter expert network that can evaluate rapid market changes and developments related to the specific company.

MCI should warn management at all levels of impending changes in the competitive landscape, including opportunity signals. This is a crucial component of corporate management in a modern, evolving economy. By analyzing the moves of other actors (customers, partners, suppliers, competitors, and regulators), MCI helps companies anticipate market development and *act accordingly, prior to competitors.*

A MCI program should deliver the following results:

- Prompt warning of competitive threats and risks
- Early identification of competitive growth opportunities
- Benchmarking of best practices
- Quicker response to market moves

- Better understanding of major players: customers, suppliers, politicians
- Future scenarios for strategic planning
- Accurate estimates for tactical decisions
- Improved development activities
- Identification of business blind spots

MCI versus business intelligence

The terms Business Intelligence (BI) and MCI are sometimes used interchangeably by intelligence practitioners. However, these labels usually mean very different things in the software business, and it is, therefore, important to distinguish between them.

- **Business Intelligence (BI)** focuses on the current internal operating environment with the goal of optimizing organizational efficiency. BI typically adopts a backward-looking stance and addresses internal, structured and/or transactional data, often in numerical form.

- **Market and Competitive Intelligence (MCI)** focuses on the external environment to identify threats and opportunities. This includes factors outside your organization, as illustrated by Porter's Five Forces[1]:

- Bargaining power of suppliers—Supplier Intelligence
- Competitive rivalry—Competitor Intelligence
- Threat of new entrants—Strategic Intelligence
- Bargaining power of customers—Customer Intelligence
- Threat of substitutes—Innovation Intelligence

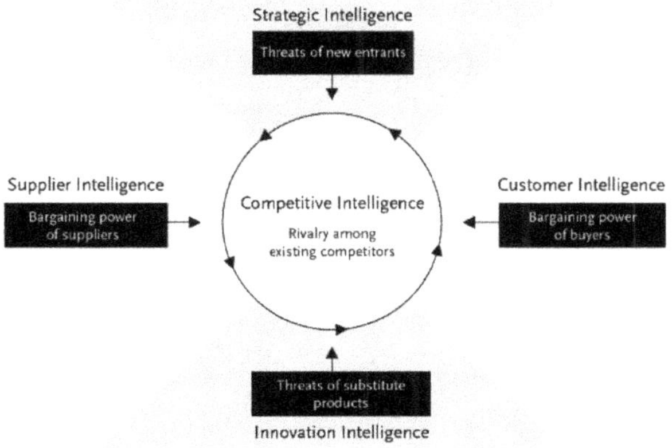

Adaption of Porter's Five Forces into Intelligence terms.

---

[1] "How Competitive Forces Shape Strategy" by Michael E. Porter, Harvard Business Review, March 1979.

MCI is future-looking and primarily addresses unstructured information, often in text format (including video and audio content conversions).

The traditional intelligence cycle

For many years, the most common way to work with competitive intelligence was the so-called "Intelligence cycle," rooted in a military concept born during the mid-1970s.

According to this model, effective competitive intelligence is a continuous cycle, encompassing the following steps:

1. Planning and Direction (collaborating with decision-makers to discover and hone their intelligence needs, deciding how to approach the designated task)
2. Collection (gathering required raw materials in a legal, ethical manner)
3. Processing and Exploitation (evaluating and organizing data)
4. Analysis and Production (interpreting data and compiling recommended actions)
5. Dissemination and Integration (reporting and presenting findings to decision-makers)

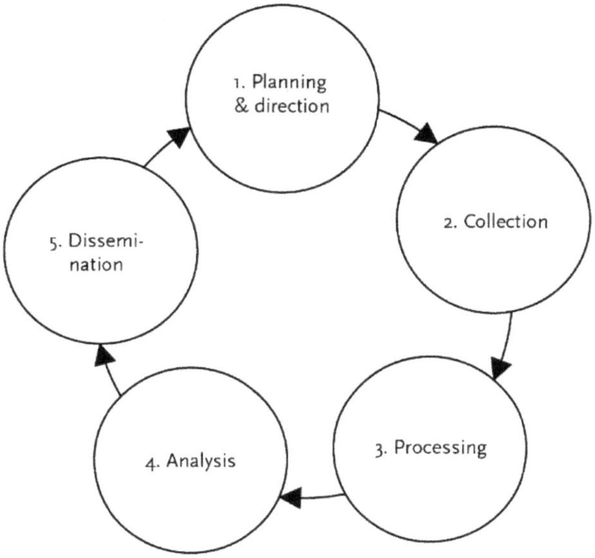

The traditional, sequential 5-Step CI Cycle.

This model may have worked when markets were relatively stable, technological advances were slower, and competitors were better defined. However, we argue this model is outdated and must be adapted to today's rapidly changing and non-hierarchical world. In Chapter 2.1, we will therefore suggest an alternative model better suited to the new VUCA world.

Success patterns and pitfalls

The success of a MCI program is unfortunately far from guaranteed just by its sheer existence. As you will find when reviewing the insights shared here, overwhelming emphasis needs to be on delivering tangible and lasting results. Quite obviously, you're reading this book to avoid joining the cohort of less-than-successful MCI initiatives. Still, it is worthwhile to reflect on standard pitfalls to be able to recognize them and act in time, should any materialize.

The success of a MCI program is unfortunately far from guaranteed just by its sheer existence.

While other explanations for failing MCI programs exist, the most common theme is an inability to impact an organization's financial bottom line and deliver results matching the organization's needs. In our experience, ineffective MCI initiatives are often implemented reactively, become unmanageable quickly, rarely deliver meaningful insight, and ultimately cease due to a lack of meaningful results delivered at the end of a budget cycle. That is, until the next surprise market event, merger, or acquisition sparks executive calls for more intelligence and better insights. Hence, unless MCI reflects true long-term capabilities, it will not succeed.

The following are five main reasons why we see CI programs fail—MCI should regularly reflect upon these to ensure they do not become a reality:

1. **Lack of purpose and target.** Without a clear understanding of why and for whom the competitive analysis is performed, the risk of failure is high.

2. **Lack of business impact.** Unless MCI leads directly to decision implementation, the value of the competitive analysis is low and the risk of failure is high.

3. **Lack of sense of urgency.** Unless the organization believes MCI is needed to survive, it is easy to continue operating in the usual manner and resist change. This will increase the risk of failure for MCI.

4. **Lack of cross-fertilization.** In siloed organizations, MCI tends to reflect the personal agendas of a chosen few. It is not enough for a small group of people detached from business operations to employ MCI.

5. **Lack of future focus.** Unless MCI deemphasizes media monitoring and past events, there is a risk of failure. To provide value, MCI must be future-focused, supporting decision-makers with early warning signals.

There is also a specific timeline development whereby a very enthusiastic early adoption may, in fact, be deceiving, having not been built on solid ground. MCI platforms are often enthusiastically implemented as a reaction to specific management needs. Companies start collecting lots of content from all sorts of places which may lead to early wins. But without a clear purpose or target, they can end up contributing to information overload with too much outdated, irrelevant information, which ultimately leads to decay

The image below illustrates what this adoption curve sometimes looks like, with high initial usage that withers unless decision makers perceive that they get business value from MCI.

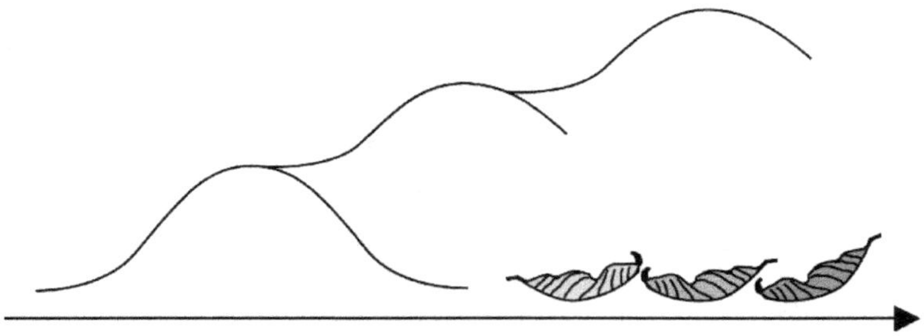

Much like the classic Technology Adaption Curve, adoption of MCI should be done step by step over time. Many failures stem from a lack of continuous innovation and value development.

Now, let's leave the failures behind, navigate around the potholes, and move forward!

Convincing executives to invest in MCI

Although we believe all organizations can benefit from an organized MCI platform, we realize many ideas and concepts in this book require resources that are often only available in larger, multinational organizations. Still, even for the smallest of operations, they can serve as concrete inspirations for long-term capabilities build-up.

When asking executives to invest in MCI, you should carefully consider the current maturity state and the intended purpose and application of your MCI platform. It must match your decision-makers' needs and expectations and realistically fulfill near-term perspectives. It is important to define the target decision-makers and which specific MCI services they need.

MCI is relevant for varied departments within an organization. It's often implemented in, and applied to, one or more of the following functions:

- Customer insights
- Marketing
- Market research
- Sales
- Product development and innovation
- Corporate strategy

Traditional reasons for investing in MCI include:

- **Saving time**, with all intelligence in one place
- **Cutting costs**, by working more efficiently and avoiding duplicate work
- **Ensuring credibility,** curating information to be relevant, reliable, and consistent
- **Delivering insight**, reaching out to everyone with intelligence needed for decision support

The reasons above are still as valid as ever, but given recent market disruptions and business environment uncertainties, there is an increased appetite for MCI to be better equipped for change: not just concerning senior management but across all parts of the organization.

Our advice is to position MCI initiatives as a learning platform that all employees can engage in to understand business strategy, market changes, and competitor moves, becoming better prepared to serve customers in the future.

Position MCI initiatives as a learning platform that all employees can engage in to understand business strategy, market changes, and competitor moves, becoming better prepared to serve customers.

This will enhance the understanding of market forces such as customers, consumer markets, and competitors—enabling you to be more creative and generate new, innovative ideas that help your organization grow and prosper in the future.

However, building a MCI capability takes time and must be constructed in a step-by-step fashion. To provide a formal ROI calculation is close to impossible due to the almost unlimited number of variables on the "revenue" side. MCI's impact on the quality of decisions is hard to quantify, though it is easier to measure efficiency in terms of time and money.

Instead, develop a long-term plan, look for incremental budget needs and suggest checkpoints after each completed step. If following this book's suggested development path, each major step and sub-steps can serve as milestones to illustrate tangible progress. The key is transparency and that all involved parties share the long-term vision and insight into the ideal evolution of the development process.

Key takeaways

Summarizing the key takeaways of this chapter:

- The pace of change is accelerating, and there is an overload of information.
- The fear of missing an important piece of the puzzle is growing and can lead to "decision paralysis."
- MCI is about systematically gathering, analyzing, and managing information about your business landscape. It helps drive decisions that improve your competitive advantage.
- MCI fails when it lacks purpose and direction.

CHAPTER 2

Everything is Changing!

Charles Darwin is said to have claimed that, "It is not the strongest of the species that survives, nor the most intelligent that survives. It is the one that is most adaptable to change." Stephen Hawking echoed this by stating that "Intelligence is the ability to adapt to change." Both Darwin and Hawking clearly had a point. Some say that we are living amidst the most extraordinary time ever in human history. In 2001, Raymond Kurzweil, the famous futurist, predicted, "We won't experience 100 years of progress in the 21st century — it will be more like 20,000 years of progress (at today's rate)."

Whatever the pace, it is obvious that the world is changing at an accelerating speed and modernized intelligence is needed now more than ever. MCI, and knowing what to do next, has never been more relevant to organizations. It further helps to ensure that change is an opportunity, not a threat, and that it will improve your position.

Organizations must become adaptive. Every day presents a situation where we might not know what lies ahead. In today's hyperactive global economy, disruptions occur at the speed of light. And now more than ever, organizations must closely monitor markets, competitors, trends, and customers to build future scenarios and roadmap alternatives to ensure their organization's success.

The key to becoming an adaptive enterprise is keeping pace with customer needs and addressing changing market requirements.

The intelligence cycle is changing

People who work with MCI are familiar with the traditional intelligence cycle as described in the previous chapter. The exact origin of the concept is unclear, and a Google search on "Intelligence Cycle" reveals many different versions. What they have in common, however, is that they describe how intelligence work is carried out:

- The cycle usually starts with a dialogue between producers and users of intelligence to identify intelligence needs.

- Planning and direction follow to create the knowledge base.

- Following data collection and processing, insights are generated and finally disseminated before the cycle stops.

The intelligence cycle is obsolete due to decentralized decision-making and non-linear information flows.

The traditional intelligence cycle works in an environment where information flows in a closed loop and tasks are distributed from the top down. Decisions are made in a strictly hierarchical order. In such settings, the intelligence professional is instructed to answer a very specific question. Put in simple terms, this takes shape as an elaborate Question and Answer (Q&A) procedure. However, today the most complex task, more often than not, is to simply ask the right questions from the get-go; for this, an entirely new model is required.

In an environment where the dialogue is iterative and non-linear, the cycle must be adapted accordingly. In today's business world, decision-making is decentralized and information flows in many directions. As organizations become flatter with more evenly distributed responsibilities, information has a tendency to lose confidentiality and is shared to a greater extent. The traditional MCI cycle assumes a dedicated MCI team that reports its insights to decision-makers who actually care and seek analysis. Today, this is seldom the case. Instead, MCI has become, or should become, a more integrated part of decision-making processes such as business development, product development, and strategic planning. MCI must support the organization's vision, strategy, and goals. Consequently, before planning and direction even begin, you need a well-defined vision and strategy from the onset. The traditional MCI cycle also lacks an important final step, which is **Actionability**. Concluding the process by simply disseminating insights and hopefully getting some feedback will not make anyone happy. In fact, it can contribute to information overload. To be of value, MCI must contribute to decision-making that transforms the organization into an adaptive organization. Based on the above, we suggest implementing an updated MCI process that aligns with today's fast-moving business world.

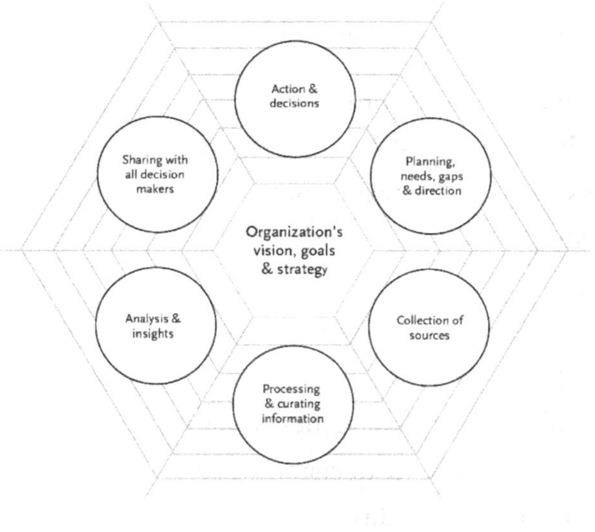

The Intelligence Web Replaces the Intelligence Cycle.

Contrary to a sequential method, the new Intelligence Web is a continuous, non-sequential web or network of information and analytics exchange that continually drives the organization and impacts corporate vision and strategy.

The Intelligence Web is a more suitable way of working in a continuous, non-sequential web or network of information and analytics exchange, always driven by corporate vision and strategy.

MCI can make sense of the increasingly fast-changing business ecosystem by developing actionable insights for the external environment. If it does this well, there will be no need to market your MCI function. Rather, it will be demanded, helping the organization understand, compete, and win in real-time while providing the basis for establishing a sustainable competitive advantage.

The competitive landscape is changing

The competitive landscape is changing due to digitalization.

"90% of the data in the world has been created in the last two years." That statement is reflected in PowerPoint slides referring to today's disruptive pace of technical innovation. It originates from a 2013 IBM analysis—and 2013 is a long time ago! Since then, the rate of data generation has increased. In fact, World Economic Forum predicts that by 2025, the amount of data generated each day is expected to reach 463 exabytes globally.

Digitalization concepts like Artificial Intelligence, Machine Learning, and Big Data are gaining traction, impacting people and businesses all over the globe. The fact that everything able to be quantified *is* quantified implies both risk and opportunity for companies. Specifically, risk of an inability to filter out irrelevant information and an opportunity to make better, faster decisions.

Companies can feel their industries getting more and more competitive. A recent survey states that the average company now has about 25 direct competitors, and according to the 1,000 business professionals who participated in the survey, it wasn't always that way; 87% shared that their market has become more competitive in the last three years, with 49 percent characterizing it as *much* more competitive.[2]

The workforce is changing

The workforce is changing due to digitalization.

---

[2] State of Competitive Intelligence, 2020, SCIP https://www.scip.org/page/StateofCompetitiveIntelligence2020.

The majority of today's workforce is comprised of Millennials, i.e., people born in the 1980s-1990s. They are maturing into leadership positions while their younger peers in Generation Z begin to come on board.

In 2020, 35% of the US workforce (some 59 million people) were freelancers.[3] A similar trend is observed in Europe, although the absolute numbers are lower. The evolving workforce demands an improved work-life balance and flexible work hours/mobility, that is, adaptable work locations.

The world is in transition

From	To
Hierarchy	Flat organizations with distributed responsibilities
Fixed work hours	Flexible work hours
Confidential information	Shared information
Manage the staff	Inspire co-workers
Wireline, fixed networks	Wireless, cloudification
Outlook, Hotmail	Snapchat, WhatsApp, Twitter, Teams, Slack, etc.
Fragmented company	Integrated, connected
Fixed workplace	Mobile workplace

Source: Comintelli analysis 2019, various web sources

---

[3] Upwork (https://www.upwork.com/press/releases/new-upwork-study-finds-36-of-the-us-workforce-freelance-amid-the-covid-19-pandemic).

The role of MCI professionals is changing

MCI professional roles are changing due to digitalization.

As mentioned previously, more information is available today than ever before. This means the amount of both useful and useless data is more abundant. At the same time, digitalization requires companies to act and make decisions much faster than ever before. Hence, as the need for perspective and knowledge increases, Market and Competitive (MCI) professionals must process more data, filter out more noise, and analyze and present insights more quickly. Another change for MCI professionals is the need to develop deeper relationships with their internal customers. This is needed to engage in more active decision-making by not only presenting facts but presenting opinions that are in line with the decision-maker's own situation and strategy. MCI professionals will act more as facilitators and less as processors.

The users and producers of intelligence are changing

All employees are becoming both consumers and producers of intelligence.

In the past, specialists performed intelligence work for a few high-ranking executives. That is rapidly changing as a wider breadth of employees convert information into insights today. Of course, varying tasks and job responsibilities impact how we work while collecting and processing data. While some focus on creating informative newsletters for the masses, others offer detailed input to support specific C-level decisions. In a recent survey, 90% of businesses said they will either increase or maintain their CI budgets[4].

The demand for self-service intelligence is increasing and many users leverage smart tools to create self-service dashboards to monitor information. MCI is also an increasingly effective way to educate all employees about the business environment. Ultimately, these "trends" fuel the content and purpose of a variety of positions. The following page contains a high-level description of how some typical job roles increasingly relate to intelligence work.

---

[4] State of Competitive Intelligence Report, 2021, SCIP (https://www.scip.org/general/custom.asp?page=2021StateofCompetitiveIntelligence).

Job Role	Typical MCI-Related Activities	MCI Target Groups	Purpose of MCI Activities
MCI Director	Plan and manage MCI projects. Budgeting. Develop and improve MCI methods, tools, and processes. Gather, analyze, prepare and present insights.	Strategy unit, Sales and Marketing unit, Account teams, Product management, C-level	Administrate and lead the MCI core team. Influence strategic planning and sales.
Market Analyst	Gather, analyze, prepare and present insights. Monitor actors, market, and trends. Prepare and distribute newsletters.	Strategy unit, Sales and Marketing unit, Account teams, Product management, C-level	Provide insights. Support strategy planning, sales, and marketing efforts.
Product Manager	Monitor actors and market. Track product developments. Prepare and distribute newsletters.	R&D unit, Product management, Sales department, C-level	Inform product strategy. Provide insights.
Customer Support Manager	Self-service intelligence. Monitor actors and market. Track product developments.	Product management, Customer	Enable services. Inform product strategy.
Account Manager	Self-service intelligence. Monitor actors, market, and trends.	Account team, Customer	Improve marketing. Enable sales. Position own company. Change pricing.

Job Role	Typical MCI-Related Activities	MCI Target Groups	Purpose of MCI Activities
Executive	Self-service intelligence. Monitor actors, market, and trends.	Self, Business area, C-level, Customer, External analysts, reporters	Improve strategy. Influence marketing. Enable sales.

Note: This list is not comprehensive.

The technology of MCI is changing

Technologies based on Artificial Intelligence will profoundly change the field of MCI.

MCI platforms have evolved tremendously in the last few years. Today, they consist of much more than just monitoring web news for events that came and went and cutting/pasting newsletters. Today's world-class MCI teams break the "MCI Cycle of Death" by leveraging technology. Recent technological advances—specifically Artificial Intelligence (AI) in the form of Natural Language Processing (NLP) and Machine Learning (ML)—offer unprecedented opportunities to automate critical but time-consuming and low-value activities of collecting, organizing, and curating information. The ideal MCI software tool allows researchers and analysts to focus on developing and enabling insights, the primary value of intelligence teams. The right tool serves as a force-multiplier for the modern MCI team, freeing the analyst from low-value tasks like collecting and organizing information.

As a sign of the times, we were delighted when the reputable and influential IT research firm Forrester formally identified and defined the MCI market in their report on Market and Competitive Intelligence platforms in Q4 2019[5] as:

"A solution that enables users to search for and analyze diverse information sources about competitors and market context by AI-assisted collection, curation, and tagging of data and information from internal and external sources. Users then leverage templates, dashboards and collaboration features to share actionable insights across their organization."

Today, no one individual can thrive within the current information and communication environment without technology support and related tools—ones that should support intelligence staff and users to visualize, make

---

[5] Source: The Forrester New Wave™: Market And Competitive Intelligence Platforms, Q4 2019 Forrester report.

sense of, and take action on insights derived from relevant information and expertise.

To provide such support, the tool must read and process huge volumes of unstructured and structured data and function to support expert network and insight dissemination with almost surgical precision. Any such tool must possess a depth of technology that is continuously updated with timely algorithms and data visualization within the industry.

Key takeaways

Summarizing the key takeaways of this chapter:

- MCI must adapt to the new fast-paced, disruptive world.
- The traditional intelligence cycle is obsolete due to decentralized decision-making and non-linear information flows.
- The Intelligence Web is a more suitable way of working in a continuous, non-sequential web or network of information and analytics exchange, always driven by corporate vision and strategy.
- Without a modern technology platform, efficient and scalable Market and Competitive Intelligence is very difficult, if not impossible.

Part II

Growing a Garden

The second part is the key part of the book (Chapters 3 and 4). We describe **what** the Garden of Intelligence is – a management concept for developing successful Market & Competitive Intelligence capabilities. The framework is a step-by-step stairway to a blooming Garden of Intelligence that will reduce your time to insights and decisions.

CHAPTER 3

Preparing the Grounds

To summarize the previous chapter, change is needed for MCI to continue to serve its purpose. The cyclical work process that prevailed since MCI evolved from military models into enterprise operations is terminally outdated. Available technology has amassed over prior decades but is not sufficiently included in MCI work. The change in organizational models developed over the same period, fueled by "social and collaboration" work processes, must be better embedded and leveraged within the MCI landscape.

This chapter introduces a framework to evolve a MCI operation from a very informal position to a "state-of the-art" capability, through six different levels.

We choose to call this framework "**The Garden of Intelligence**," as we believe Market and Competitive Intelligence capabilities must evolve step by step and develop with care, patience, and agility. There is no "Big Bang" solution, and it will not happen overnight using magic AI robots. Rather, grit, time, resources, and perseverance are required. Much like in the gardening world, the minute you forget to water your plants, provide nutrients, trim branches, and weed your garden, plants will wither and decay. The same applies to your MCI platform.

This part of the book describes the framework of six different levels to ultimately grow a "Garden of Intelligence." Cultivating a beautiful garden that will thrive for generations is not only time-consuming but takes grit, experience, and perseverance. The gardeners are exposed to the evolution of the six levels on a step-by-step basis: defining where to start, building a structure, understanding sources, understanding decision-maker needs and forging connections, applying analytics, and finally, embedding MCI operations within all decision-making processes throughout the organization.

The phases and levels of growing a Garden of Intelligence

A blooming *Garden of Intelligence* is developed in six phases, leading to six respective levels of maturity, as described below.

The fact that the phases and levels are numbered from one to six does not imply they must be carried out in chronological order. Rather, it is likely that while addressing one level, others are also involved in varied iterative ways. The key is not to jump too far ahead without maintaining a solid foundation. After all, it is impossible to grow a tree from a seed if you do not nurture the soil in the process.

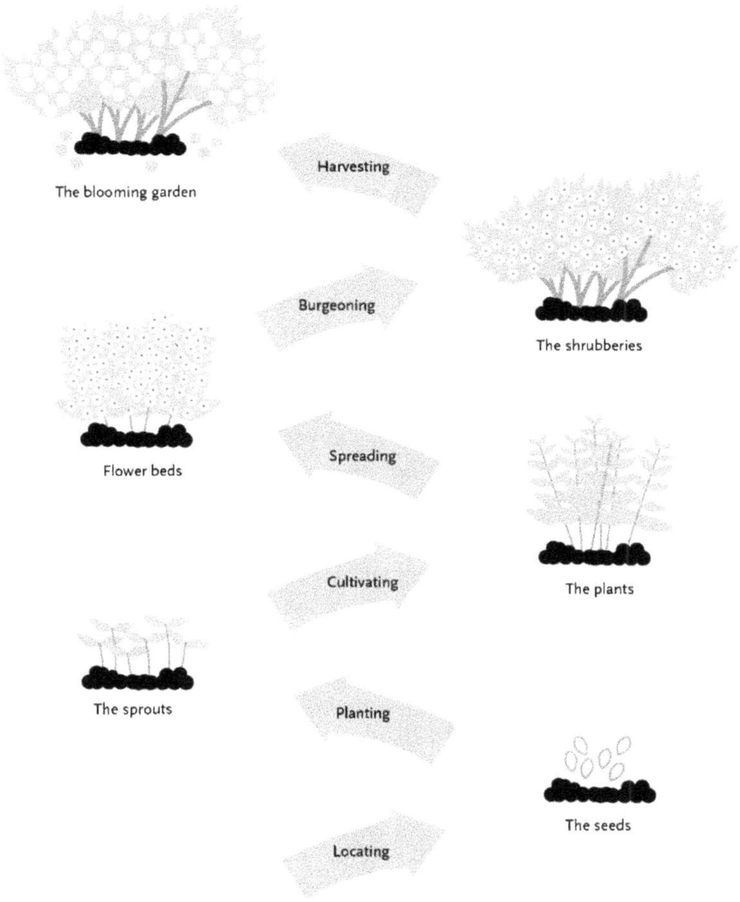

Evolving through the six phases and six levels of a Garden of Intelligence.

	Phases	Levels
	**Phase A—Locating** You are mapping out your garden of intelligence, evaluating its terrain, soil, and weather conditions. This will bring you to the very first level of your design.	**Level 1: The Seeds**—You realize that the organization will benefit from a better understanding of its business environment. You have surveyed tools and procedures already in place. You know where to start and have secured the first seeds.
	**Phase B—Planting** This is when you plant the first seeds and truly embark on the journey to develop your garden of intelligence. It is the phase that will be most visible to passersby. Something entirely new, tangible, and beautiful is growing. This phase leads to Level 2.	**Level 2: The Sprouts**—You have constructed your first MCI structure and connected open-source feeds. Your team is still small, but usage is growing.
	**Phase C—Cultivating** Your garden is now attracting attention, and you must cater to more visitors. By laying out new paths and organizing your sprouts, you granularize biodiversity and enable a more targeted experience for botanically mindful visitors. By further cultivating each section specifically for each sprout species, you spur growth into hardy plants.	**Level 3: The Plants**—You have boosted MCI usage numbers. Internal sources are now included in the system, and you add external commercial sources such as news and analysis providers.

	Phases	Levels
	**Phase D—Spreading** You now have a garden with all basic plants in place. You are happy with the design and the harmony it provides, but it is still fragile. Plants and trees need more nutrition, with some requiring supporting plants to shield them from heightened sun exposure. Others might need better irrigation. You are now honing the details, leading to subsequent levels.	**Level 4: The Flower Beds**—You have welcomed decision-makers into the workflow. The focus is now on delivering business benefits to all MCI users. Users have become involved as MCI observers in information-collection processes.
	**Phase E—Burgeoning** Your garden is, in all material respects, fully grown. Plants, flowers, and trees are firmly rooted in the ground. The varieties are many, and the beauty is there for everyone to enjoy. A walk in your garden will inspire confidence and new thoughts. Your work as a gardener is now to ensure a stable and long-term maintenance of the garden.	**Level 5: The Shrubberies** — With all information now at hand, you apply more advanced analytics and share results with managers and strategists throughout the organization. MCI is inspiring and enabling dialogue per such analysis.
	**Phase F—Harvesting** Time to reap the real benefits of perseverance as well as both structured and intense development work. By ensuring all visitors and contributors to your garden are constantly aware of its growing beauty and development from season to season, your creation will endure. Ongoing cultivation will guarantee a bountiful harvest in the years to come, bringing your garden to the final level of its maturity evolution.	**Level 6: The Blooming Garden**—You have fulfilled your development ambitions. MCI is now a firmly embedded component within management responsibilities in both line and project organizations.

The Information, Technology, People (ITP) framework

To describe proper MCI management across the six different levels, we will use a conceptual model for socio-technical analysis of related processes that identifies three mutually interdependent perspectives:

- Information (I)
- Technology (T)
- People (P)

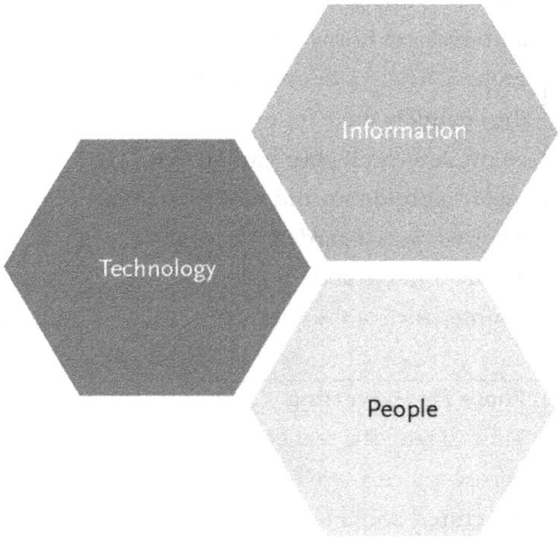

These are loosely based on the phrase "People, Process, and Technology," which originates from Harold Leavitt's well-established 1964 paper, "Applied Organization Changes in Industry." In it, he presents a widely accepted four-part "Diamond" model to create organizational change.

Information (I)

Information consists of data arranged in some order (for instance, by classification or rational presentation) to acquire meaning or reveal associations between data items. Information is applied by Technology and used by People.

Many sources can supply this information, divided into two main types:

- **External information**—From any sources outside of the organization, e.g., published reports, magazines or trade journals, and anything on the web

- **Internal information**—From any sources within the organization, e.g., proprietary presentations, documents and surveys, internal e-mail exchanges, or remarks made by employees

Technology (T)

In this context, Technology means using computers to store, retrieve, transmit and manipulate information, typically used within the context of business operations.

People work with these tools. Technology helps people structure information and execute faster, more innovative work—especially in the age of Artificial intelligence.

People (P)

People are the humans working together and performing tasks to achieve organizational goals. People, by themselves, have to do work. How they perform and apply work is key. Even in the age of Artificial Intelligence, *people* must govern the output of machines (for now).

Process helps people do better work, defining and standardizing it to prevent a need to reinvent the wheel.

Harmonizing ITP

If any of these three ITP components are missing, our experience is that MCI will ultimately fail. Rapidly developing the "people capability" without supporting technology and information access is as futile as heavily investing in advanced software tools with no one available to draw conclusions. It is a perfect example of the saying that no chain is stronger than its weakest link.

The three ITP components must develop gradually, together, to eventually reach an intelligence capability that will truly contribute to the organization's competitiveness. Consequently, deploying a MCI platform in an organization is a long-term commitment that involves developing a number of resources and capabilities. Over time, these evolve into one holistic approach, but, as always, one must start from the beginning. Consequently, the guide for leveling up your garden is presented with this ITP model as a foundation.

The team of gardeners

To undertake the activities outlined in this chapter, you will need to surround yourself with a team of gardeners. Growing a garden is *not* a one-person job! Gardener duties and responsibilities can, for example, include maintaining and mowing lawns, monitoring watering needs of the grounds under their care, pruning trees and shrubs, monitoring plant health problems, applying fertilizers and weed-control agents, maintaining gardening equipment and tools, and much, much more.

We will primarily introduce and discuss the varied activities from the perspective of a "Director of MCI," but all roles defined below reflect their own "list of activities." Each organization has its own take on how to build teams, so the below suggested team setup is not cast in stone. Just ensure you allocate the duties and responsibilities to someone in one way or another.

The team of gardeners should comprise the following six roles:

1. Executive Sponsor—Owner of the garden
2. Director of MCI—Lead gardener

3. Information specialists—Looks after the seeds and plants
4. Technology specialist—Tends to the equipment and tools
5. Analysts—Applies fertilizers and water the garden
6. Decision-makers—Consumers of the garden produce

Executive Sponsor

The Executive Sponsor is the "owner of the garden," so to speak. This is a key decision-maker who is a primary consumer of intelligence.

Often, this role is a C-suite executive (e.g., CEO, Chief Strategy Office, CMO, or COO) or even on the board level. The Director of MCI often reports to this person. This role is normally not so active in actually growing the garden, but crucial for initiating the garden in the first place—and an avid consumer of everything the garden grows, as well!

Director of MCI

This is the person assigned the marvelously inspiring, rewarding, and demanding mandate of growing the organization's MCI capabilities.

In the everyday development work of growing a Garden of Intelligence, this is the "Lead Gardener," the lead strategist, community leader, and, most importantly, MCI communicator and ambassador within the organization. This means he or she is often responsible for the "People" component of ITP. A key role requirement is that it is staffed by a person who thoroughly understands the industry, marketplace, and company culture. We, therefore, recommend recruiting internally to fulfill this role. An important step for the Director of MCI is to build the team of gardeners, as described below.

Information specialists

Since information sourcing is a critical part of MCI, an information specialist is a must. They are responsible for looking after the content of the garden, ensuring the right seeds are planted.

This role summons a broad spectrum of choices, including a recent MBA with a background in your industry/time spent with your organization, a digital library professional, someone with an industry-relevant research background, or the like. The key characteristic is a proven understanding of the "content industry," both free and paid sources, and a solid understanding of internal company sources, i.e., business-supporting processes and internal knowledge management systems. This is a role that will have to develop over time.

Naturally, this is often the person responsible for the "Information" component of ITP.

Technology specialists

Technology specialists are responsible for all IT-related matters. This can include hardware and software platforms, policy and security compliance, and integration with other systems. They are the ones who look after the equipment and tools used in the garden.

A key capability for this role is someone who understands the current organization's IT environment. He or she need not be a programmer but rather a system architect with a deeply rooted interest in business strategy. Naturally, this is often the role responsible for the "Technology" component of ITP.

Analysts

Analysts are responsible for reviewing information, identifying what is relevant, and putting it into the context of their organization. They develop conclusions for likely courses of action and provide recommendations for decision-makers.

You will find analysts throughout your organization in marketing, sales, and product development teams, corporate headquarters, strategy groups, etc. A common trait is that a senior manager has tasked them to "keep me informed about the market, please."

Analysts add fertilizer and water the garden so that plants bear fruit; be mindful of analysts when evolving your MCI capabilities, as they represent the core network of your MCI operation and serve as primary insight producers. Only a few analysts will likely be present when your garden is conceived, but the group will rapidly expand if it is managed well.

Decision-makers

These are your garden visitors and consumers, the widest role you must consider, by far. These are your user representatives who truly understand how MCI processes and output exert a bottom-line impact on business decisions.

Involve them early on as your "tasting" team to sample the fruits of your garden. When developing new garden outputs (i.e., MCI services), employ a few decision-makers as "tasters." They will serve as the ultimate judges for the quality of your produce. MCI's impact on decision-makers is the primary justification for growing your garden in the first place.

Key takeaways

Summarizing the key takeaways of this chapter:

- The six maturity levels of the Garden of Intelligence are:

    1. The Seeds
    2. The Sprouts
    3. The Plants
    4. The Flower Beds
    5. The Shrubberies
    6. The Blooming Garden

- The Information, Technology, People framework is key for managing your Garden of Intelligence.

- The team of gardeners should comprise the following six roles:

    1. Executive Sponsor—Owner of the garden
    2. Director of MCI—Lead gardener
    3. Information specialists—Look after the seeds and plants
    4. Technology specialist—Tends to the equipment and tools
    5. Analysts—Apply fertilizers and water the garden
    6. Decision-makers—Garden produce consumers

Now that we have prepared the grounds, we are ready to go and work our garden!

CHAPTER 4

The Six Levels of a Garden of Intelligence

This chapter describes the six different levels and corresponding development phases for your blooming Garden of Intelligence. This is the key portion of this book and serves as the inspiration, targeting support, and fundamental project structure for a team of gardeners tasked with embedding a state-of-the-art MCI operation within an organization.

We are about to unveil the six levels for growing a Garden of Intelligence, but first, let's introduce how each level is described using the following four perspectives:

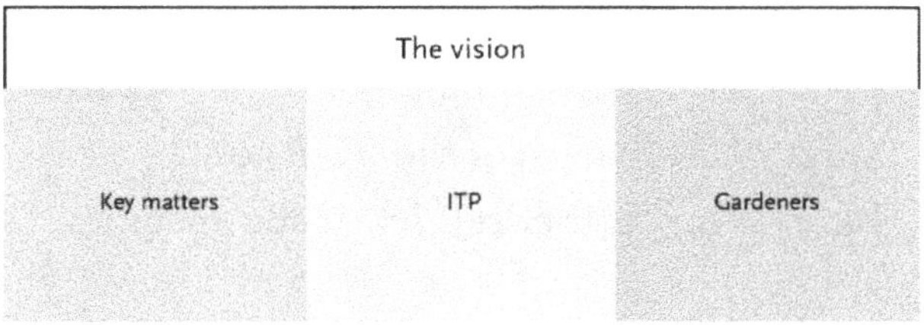

The vision of each level (Where?) is accomplished by following What? (Key Matters), How? (Information, Technology, People) and Who? (Gardeners tasks).

1. ***The Vision – Where are your going?*** When you have achieved the targeted level, which benefits will you claim right then and there? This is a description of your achievements and their associated impact(s).

2. ***Key Matters – What needs to be done?*** This serves as an introduction with a bulleted list of questions and issues, outlining tasks that are central for level progression. These may differ from organization to organization and across varied company cultures but are important to monitor as the levels develop and for continued nurturing when new ones are achieved. The remainder of each section should support the execution of this material, but you may very well need "cultural tuning" within your organization from time to time.

3. ***Information, Technology, People (ITP) – How will it be done?*** Concrete development tasks and actions are described based on the IT (Information-Technology-People) framework presented in the previous chapter. The ITP structure is also represented in the "Digging Deeper" portion of the book, wherein each of the I/T/P contains two chapters for further reference and insights.

4. ***Gardener Tasks – Who should do it?*** The gardeners introduced in the previous chapters will be kept busy for the duration of development. This perspective is to understand better what each role

must focus on and initiate. You will also find comments on ongoing responsibilities needed to maintain levels already achieved while preparing to advance to those ahead.

This should provide a solid understanding of goals and how to advance to each new level. When setting out to level up from one point to the next, do consult the relevant chapters of Part III, "Digging Deeper", to find more elaborate descriptions of the Garden of Intelligence model.

- Chapters 5 and 6 are about Information—Structure and Sources
- Chapters 7 and 8 are about Technology—Today and in the Future
- Chapters 9 and 10 are about People—How to Connect and Build Adaptable Mindsets.

Locating: Evolving to Level 1—The Seeds

The vision

As its starting point, our framework considers an organization where some individuals suddenly realize enhanced marketplace knowledge is a great idea.

They accept that work is required to achieve this, and the organization creates the first embryo for a team of gardeners. You have the seeds, and you believe you know where to plant them.

Key matters

A typical starting point for "development" towards this level is that informally organized strategy and business analysts collaborate and share thoughts on where they are/where they should be heading. Questions discussed might include:

- Are we in a rapidly changing industry?
- Are there disruptions?
- Do new competitors exist?
- Can we effectively manage all information?
- Are we suffering from information overload?

- Is most of our work ad-hoc, via e-mail, with little coordination or structure?
- Is management on board, understanding the benefits with the right expectations?
- Does our business understand the value of market and competitor intelligence?
- Is there a sense of decision-maker urgency that intelligence is needed?
- Which area(s) of our organization seek an MCI platform, if at all?
- Which business outcomes are we looking for, or enabling others to seek out?

The typical outcome of these processes is a final key question: How do we inject some structure into these trains of thought to launch impactful initiatives?

Information, Technology, People (ITP)

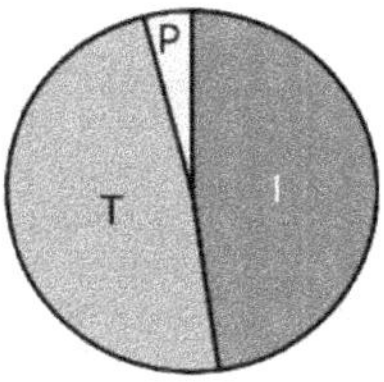

Share of work in the Locating phase – most of the work starts with Information and Technology.

Many roadblocks may exist at this level. The key common denominator is where the organization finds itself when the level is reached, i.e., accepting to do more in a more structured way. The ITP discussion below is therefore very indicative as a first step in the process of formalizing the forthcoming work.

INFORMATION	At this level, the organization places little if any focus on the information strategy. Identifying the need for "the something" is more than enough. The typical starting point is deploying more or less rudimentary technology solutions to gather information that might already exist within the organization. Some may utilize information services such as Google alerts, only to soon realize the sheer volume of data combined with a lack of structure makes this an impossible task. For these enthusiasts, it is merely a question of "mapping" and understanding their immediate surroundings to understand the application of existing knowledge.
TECHNOLOGY	The team will likely find the organization boasts shared folders within its SharePoint (or equivalent) environment for general "document sharing purposes," but with limited thoughts on leveraging any insights. It is also likely that some scattered junior marketing employees who are unaware of one another are responsible for "keeping track of and storing market news." Other tools used are e-mail newsletters, Google alerts, and attempts to gather internal documents on an ad-hoc basis. This is essentially a very preliminary "as-is map" of current capabilities to be crafted, no more. They may not even realize where they are heading until they are deeply ingrained within this level.

PEOPLE	Thoughts about formal MCI organization, or MCI people management, tend to not yet exist, but an enthusiastic team may be excited to tell colleagues and managers they are onto something. Bravo! Do whatever you can to spread this enthusiasm, as it will help tremendously when it comes time to take more formal action towards the next level.

Gardener tasks

Even if formal team roles are not yet established, their *tasks* will be. Approach the task descriptions below from the perspective that the final result will exist as an awareness and preliminary plan for steps required to reach the next level.

Director of MCI

Someone will inevitably adopt the role of spearheading development and bring the team together, closer to a more formal work group. It is likely this person, later on, will be assigned the mandate outlined in Section 3.2 that he or she is labeled "Director of MCI." Building up towards "The Seeds" level, the Director energizes and communicates within the team. This person may be scattered within the actual work, trying hard to assign structure to all initiatives. He or she should focus on two specific tasks:

- Document all thoughts and insights into one format in preparation for the next steps

- To the best of his/her ability, prepare executives for the road ahead, requesting to form a development project and building awareness

Information specialist

The information source specialist should already thrive in this development phase. Do your best to document as much as you can regarding the use and production of existing market-related information. Try to identify common denominators regarding types of external sources and their usage. These preliminary results will suffice to support the Director's development specification draft as grounds for more detailed evaluations moving forward.

Technology specialist

The IT specialist will work with initial mapping for the current IT environments rather than sources. For the purpose of modeling, draft and document some simple use-cases that can serve as decision support for the upcoming project and a starting point for more detailed elaboration in the next development phases.

Analysts

It is likely that all team members are fascinated by business analytics, but you should assign one person as the primary "analyst" from the get go. Moving forward, this person will consolidate all insights regarding analytical models and procedures used in the organization, information crucial for the team for future levels.

Decision-makers

It is highly likely that all individuals above, more or less, currently serve as their own decision-makers with enthusiasm grounded in an ability to tackle problems encountered in their daily work. This role will emerge in later levels.

Planting: Evolving to Level 2—The Sprouts

The vision

With your Sprouts in place, the work of developing MCI is now visible to observers. A system and a structure are in place, and a standardized use of external sources has commenced.

MCI is in its first level of maturity, whereby some actual business impact is detected. At the Sprouts level, a sense of deep satisfaction within the MCI community should exist. This achievement is a big first step towards the future.

Key matters

Once you have secured the location of and seeds for your garden, you should begin planting. Structure, language, sources, and tools are required to grow them into Sprouts. These nutrients may seem somewhat cumbersome to establish, but as you will see, it is really just a matter of taking things step by step. This is the most crucial phase of development as the foundation for subsequent steps. Without Sprouts, there would be nothing to cultivate despite irrigation and nurturing. When evolving from Seeds to Sprouts, key matters to address include:

- Have a plan with a purpose!
- Who needs insights, and what are their expectations?
- Consider the sources required. Focus on open, external sources. Effective news monitoring is a "low-hanging fruit."
- Select software that can cater to your target level in the long term.
- Define which sources, topics, tags, and facets are important to you.
- Weave all of the above into your first platform. This is very important, yet only the first step.
- Launch the platform for a smaller group of core users.

Information, Technology, People (ITP)

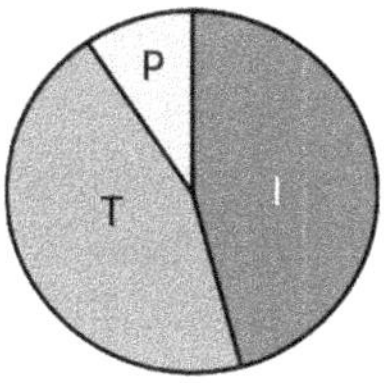

Share of work in the Planting phase - the largest share of the work is still in Information and Technology.

Contrary to the ITP in the previous phase, a solid project plan to follow should now exist. Hence, the following are recommended contents of such for this phase.

INFORMATION	In this phase, focus on two key elements of the information perspective: the initial external *sources* and the fundamental structure, the *taxonomy*. Sources—In This Step, Specifically, External Sources Any initial review of a MCI operation will include the question, "What sources do you use?" Every industry has its own universe of sources/experts, and how a MCI operation chooses to employ these is a main differentiator between successful and not-so-successful results. How to choose external sources, however, is a topic of its own (see Chapter 6), but a suggested start is to leverage open-source content in combination with a limited volume of licensed, but inexpensive, information to ultimately get the operation off the ground with enough information to fine-tune related activities and tools. Taxonomies Fundamentally, a taxonomy is a classification system—a standardized and controlled set of topics, terms, and phrases. Taxonomies have historically enjoyed a large role in biology, such as for plant and animal classification. Library sciences uses taxonomies to classify books according to a structure that makes them easy to find. Taxonomies in a business context serve a similar purpose but are used to categorize information to facilitate storing and retrieval. As information is primarily used to support or improve decision-making, a taxonomy should enable procedures to minimize time spent seeking required information and considering all relevant information when making decisions. In this sense, view taxonomies as decision-support tools. It is fair to say that a folder structure (e.g., shared network

	drives) is one possible representation of a taxonomy, but in the context of today's business needs, this is an insufficient approach. In a modern business context, design taxonomies for "tagging." Taxonomy development is a team effort with varied aspects to consider when embarking on this task. First, as you are an MCI team, ensure you work with a *context*-based, rather than a *content*-based, taxonomy (see Chapter 5). Also, keep in mind that technology can do a lot for you. A good idea is to do this alongside your first software trial. AI algorithms, Machine Learning, and models for manual configurations of automation algorithms are typically good sounding boards when developing a detailed structure.
TECHNOLOGY	When initiating a MCI development project, procure a supporting software application. There is simply no way around it, given the massive amount of information to be processed and analyzed. There are a handful of MCI purpose-built software packages available today. Some are very versatile and adaptable to your forthcoming development, while others support a vendor-specific work process. You may prefer to employ the latter in this first step to reduce the variables, but beware this can become significantly more expensive down the road as your requirements change and the software cannot follow suit. We recommend laying out a long-term development plan and assess tools from your attempted goal(s) perspective. Use this book as a guide to provide insight on which tools you need to achieve a full, blooming Garden of Intelligence. Also, keep in mind that just because you employ a

	comprehensive package at the onset does not mean you must utilize every single feature from Day One. Instead, it provides the potential to evolve gradually. For a more in-depth review of software selection procedures, see Chapter 7.
PEOPLE	This level is almost entirely Information and Technology-focused. Even in the face of ongoing communication with the upcoming MCI constituencies, user focus must remain on the I and T of the ITP approaching this level. We will introduce the people perspective later on.

Gardener tasks

Director of MCI

The Director is now the formal project manager for development towards the Sprouts vision. There are two specific areas to deliver under the watch of the Director:

- Produce a plan for where you want your MCI operation to be in 24 to 36 months. Make sure to include measurable milestones to communicate with those allocating budgets for development. A good practice is to assign the garden framework levels as milestones to monitor.

- Develop the taxonomy as set out with I in ITP above. This is by far the most important activity for those in this phase of development. Get the taxonomy wrong and the entire project will likely fail. The taxonomy is the lens for your entire business environment and the structure to build forthcoming insight processes. See also "Digging Deeper" in Chapter 5. It is good to do this in parallel to software evaluation, as taxonomy requirements can influence those for the software.

Information specialist

In this phase, the information source specialist focuses on two key tasks:

- Review sources as set out under I in ITP above, defining what you would like to include in your first set-up and estimating a budget for your plan period (this should not take more than a week or two to complete).

- Support the Director with taxonomy development, something he or she will surely appreciate.

Technology specialist

The IT specialist must fulfill two crucial tasks to complete development to the Sprouts:

- Select software that can cater to the goal level in 24 to 36 months, not just a short-term solution for the next year. Do not rush this process—allocating two to four months for selection and evaluation is not unusual before making a procurement decision.

- Once procured, configure software with the taxonomy and sources, making it operational for initial MCI activity.

Analysts

The analyst can continue mapping analysis models and procedures to prepare for subsequent levels and rolling out more coordinated analysis, but the key tasks in approaching the Sprouts level are:

- Contribute to taxonomy development
- Deploy all experiences for analytics mapping to help taxonomy development procedures
- Craft taxonomies in a team environment, fostering discussion and varied perspectives

Decision-makers

During the development phase, it is highly likely that the team will slowly attract attention from forward-looking business managers. Embrace these as they represent your first decision-makers. Involve them in the taxonomy development.

Cultivating: Evolving to Level 3—The Plants

The vision

Your Sprouts have now grown into proper Plants. A solid plant is much stronger and can withstand external pressure, so it is now much more likely to survive the test of time.

Both internal sources and users are now formally part of the MCI operation. When surveyed, it contributes measurably to the organization's business results, and there are recognized value and satisfaction in its services.

Key matters

First and foremost, good news! If nurturing your Seeds to Sprouts felt cumbersome (and it is), cultivating them to Plants is much more straightforward. The Seeds planting phase is a large undertaking, with varied developments that must work in tandem from the start to reach the Sprouts level. With the fundamental platform and processes now in place (the Sprouts are visible, remember), we can proceed in a more step-by-step manner. To nurture your MCI operation into Plants, you must:

- Expand the breadth of external content, utilizing social media and licensed premium content
- Connect internal and primary sources
- Conduct a security review and, if necessary, add layers of access rights, authentication, and roles to your MCI IT solution
- Engage your business colleagues by adding additional recipients for your deliverables. Launch your alert notification service. Heavily market the platform to gain users, and thereby, ambassadors and new decision-makers.

Information, Technology, People (ITP)

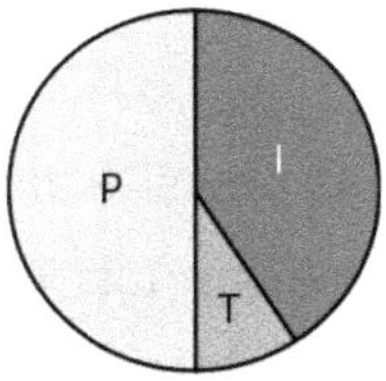

Share of work in the Cultivating phase – People requires more effort along with Information.

You are now on the development track and should know how to apply the ITP guidance provided herein. Let's discuss some specifics as you look to grow from Sprouts to Plants.

INFORMATION

Like the previous phase, this one contains a significant focus on information. Step up external sources while employing a structured approach for internal ones.

External sources

Gathering information is not a challenge these days, as its ubiquitous in most industries. Rather, the challenge is to cull *relevant* information and consciously select and manage sources to narrow down the target information to a digestible volume of useful content. Therefore, let's start with external source expansion.

For those unaware, there is actually a content market *about* the content market. This speaks to the importance of these matters and the accumulated volume of costs incurred by companies that employ intelligence professionals.

There are two major categories of external sources:

- Open sources such as the web, news sources, and social media.
- Commercial sources such as analysis companies and news bureaus.

How one chooses to mix these sources significantly impacts output and required work volume/costs. To progress to the Plants level, we suggest you take the "final step" concerning licensed content and review your basic level content strategy once more, now that you understand how systems and processes operate within your organization. Again, consult "Digging Deeper" in Chapter 6.

<u>Internal sources</u>

A major new capability to add in this step is leveraging internal sources. Any company can procure and connect external sources to a MCI system, and even if your taxonomy and automation algorithms are the best for your decision support, internal sources simply cannot be duplicated and provide a true competitive advantage.

There are two categories for internal sources: *content and people*. Yes, people create internal content, but keep reading, and you'll see why we make that distinction following ITP-People.

Most companies have massive amounts of information stored in SharePoint environments, CRM systems, LAN drives and other repositories, depending on current legacy environments. Consider two questions:

a) Which repositories include information to support your intelligence operation's key focus?
b) Which systems represent the repository of choice for colleagues working with market data and market understanding?

Contact your IT department and request permission to connect your MCI system to those repositories. Then, import data on an ongoing basis in the same way you do now with external information, including customer insights, their needs, and potential competitive challenges that may be noted by your sales team in your CRM system.

TECHNOLOGY	This phase is much less focused on the technology perspective than the previous phase, but two very important factors are quality and security. As you add

	more "non-MCI-users" to your community, requirements for quality assessed information will also increase. There are varied ways of doing this within different systems, depending on each MCI team's internal procedures. Further, when inviting more users to share and comment, ensure your MCI system fulfills internal security requirements such as Single Sign On (SSO) so users feel secure that their contributions are safe with the MCI team.
PEOPLE	Engaging people in an organization to support MCI is not a trivial task. Anyone who has tried knows this takes time, often a long time, and dictates MCI team commitment to succeed. However, we can start by providing two very well substantiated pieces of advice: a) Any attempt based on required reporting, including expected weekly competitor mail to MCI, such as to provide input for an executive letter, will, in most cases, rapidly fail. You may initially receive some quality material, but in four to eight months, the river dries up due to "lacking feedback." b) Contrary to a) above, attempts based on MCI providing users with useful information *and then* asking for feedback or support have a much higher likelihood for long-term success. A frequent experience is those who start with a smaller team of users and gradually grow the involved community are more likely to succeed than those who try to involve everyone at the same time. There are many reasons for this, but the bottom line is that it seems to work. Engaging your colleagues as "observers" (read more about this in Chapter 6) to round up internal views on

market developments is essential for a capable MCI operation. No central or even distributed MCI team can ever rise to the collective understanding and knowledge of the combination of your colleagues.

So, where to start? This is a big task! We suggest you take the easiest way forward and introduce your MCI system's personalized alerting function to your colleagues. Do not procure a system without this feature! Record a simple instruction video for your MCI system and reach out to the first team of colleagues you wish to engage. Soon after, others will contact you and ask to join the alerted groups. For you as the MCI team, this will provide a wealth of information on how to proceed and enable you to follow up on what your colleagues are seeking when setting up alerts. With the alerting function rolled out, requesting various types of comments is not such a hard sell. Now, you have established an actual dialogue with your users and may eventually inspire some of them to help originate content directly for your MCI environment. Familiarize yourself with Chapter 9 for more thoughts on this topic.

Gardener tasks

Director of MCI

This is the phase wherein the Director's communicative skill will face its first major test. Focus entirely on the P component of ITP and leave the I and T to your colleagues. Specifically:

- Ensure your MCI users *start using the tool* and develop your team's capability to support selected decision-makers with one-to-one briefs, newsletters, and analysis, all according to your intended MCI service for your initial users.

- As early as possible, introduce a more focused approach to align decision-makers as your reference group and involve them in development discussions.

Information specialist

Complete the I component of the ITP:

- Start by revising and extending the use of external and licensed content.

- Plan and connect the internal sources of your choice.

- When those two pieces are ready, wait for a month and review the quality of system content. If insufficient, reiterate until you are satisfied with the result.

Technology specialist

When leaving the Sprouts level behind, the IT specialist can shift focus to peripheral tasks. The system is in place and IT competence is a crucial support function, but the primary job function is done (for some time). Typically, though, this is a good time to:

- Tackle the T component of ITP and conduct a security review of the system, adding required layers of security if necessary
- Plan for wider systems training among users

Analysts

Reach out and make yourselves known. Start producing regular MCI news, advice and "provoke" MCI dialogue in the business process. One specific action that will make a huge impact is to invite the first team of colleagues to receive your alerts, initiating the dialogue suggested above

Decision-makers

The decision-maker's role is becoming more concrete during this level, and the task is essentially the same from here onwards: deploy a preferred level of MCI capabilities in the ongoing business operations, in turn continuously testing them in "real-life" business use cases. Ongoing feedback for MCI development is imperative, enabling it to tune in according to actual needs.

Spreading: Evolving to Level 4—The Flower Beds

The vision

Flowers everywhere! MCI has reached the level of true impact on company business. Executives and decision-makers, in general, begin to require MCI as part of their decision processes.

The MCI profession and network are gaining an internal reputation. MCI is now a well-established and targeted analytics service operation beyond the more information provisioning basis that existed at previous levels.

Authors' note: Congratulations on reaching this level—further than many organizations ever accomplish!

Key matters

Already at the Plants level, you have a firm capability to support decisions within your organization. Perhaps you even possess a truly well-oiled intelligence machine that is highly knowledgeable about the market and looming necessary strategy changes. The big question at such a level is, *Does MCI really have an impact on the organization?*

Unless your MCI capability is put to the test with real-time decision-making, it is truly of no actual value and hence still constantly at risk of being dismantled. Any decision-maker requires targeted, precise information, and the risk at the Plants level is that MCI remains a general aggregator of news and insights. Your foundation for reaching the Flower Beds is, however, very solid. You already boast a fully automated platform, spending minimal time collecting information, managing large volumes of data, and optimizing your time for analysis, reflection, and communication. Evolving to the next level means you must now support your organization's intelligence needs with enhanced precision and accessibility. Typical capabilities to nurture your Plants into proper Flower Beds include:

- Manage ever-larger volumes of content
- Differentiate your target groups and enable distributed ownership of platform components to varied parts of the organization that run their own dashboards
- Develop profiles and/or templates for your analysis targets (e.g., battle cards for sales reps)
- Introduce benchmarking as a holistic tool for strategy and decision-making
- Spread adoption of the platform's mobile interface

- Extend alerts to a much wider audience

Keep in mind that your garden is now at a level wherein it may differ from others depending on soil, geography, sun, etc., so more and more, you must consider natural growth factors within your specific habitat, your organization. Hence, the following must be considered more of an ala carte menu of suggested actions rather than concrete advice as shared for previous development phases.

Information, Technology, People (ITP)

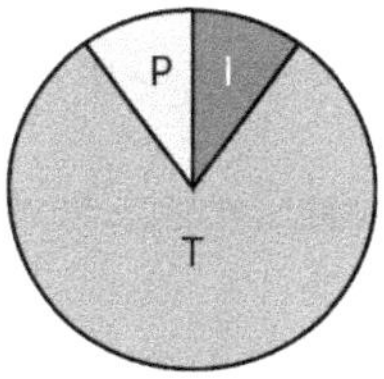

Share of work in the Spreading phase - the largest share of the work is in Technology.

INFORMATION	This development phase is more or less entirely focused on scalability and impact. That is, making use of your now implemented and proven technology to *reach out*. Varied modes of information connect to your platform, so the only remaining challenge is to match newly identified needs with potential new sources if needed. Hence, as the user group or analysis scope expands, always revisit the sourcing specifications to secure relevant input to the system.

TECHNOLOGY	You have now reached the point in your development where you will be thankful you did not choose a budget solution for your MCI technology. The following are five suggested value drivers you can implement with relative ease if you have secured your Plant status: • Differentiate target groups and work with dashboards • Add intelligence templates • Add specific tools such as benchmarks and battle cards • Promote mobile/smartphone access to MCI system • Extend alerting use to a greater extent These are described in further detail below. <u>Differentiate target groups and work with dashboards</u> The first thing to do is define your target group subsets. We are examining all work from the same information base, so it all boils down to varied techniques used to slice and dice the content. A capable MCI system will feature well-developed functionality for designing dashboards that accommodate varied user needs. Try to define at least five archetype decision-makers, and invite two or three from each to a dialogue on how a personalized MCI system dashboard would best serve them. With a small team of satisfied decision-makers as your "MCI customers," the news of your services will spread like wildfire.

Add intelligence templates

You will soon experience requests for structured formats to deliver base facts and news, and the key word is recognizability. That is, if a decision-maker receives information about a customer or competitor, it shall be structured identically to any other similar content he or she was presented with before. Templates are the tool of choice here. Amass your best company, market, and product strategists and agree on how to best analyze and present facts and findings of an organization, market, or product, putting that to work in your MCI platform.

Add specific tools such as benchmarks and battle cards

You can expand the type of templates deployed in any way you like. A popular profile type is that of "battle cards," typically used by sales reps and teams when positioning your organization against competitors in sales meetings and processes. Benchmarking provides another valuable use of profile-based information. With such structured data at hand, decision-makers can easily compare developments, strengths, weaknesses, and other factors over a range of interest areas to gain a more holistic understanding.

Promote mobile/smartphone access to MCI system

Many employees work remotely or are constantly on the move. A mobile interface is required to support not only your sales teams but any decision-maker who now encounters your MCI platform.

	<u>Extend the use of alerts</u> Make sure to conclude Phase 4 by extending your "alerts strategy." Make sure to develop a library of suggested alerts. Record new instruction videos for decision-making, not just MCI itself. Develop the alerting function into a corporate MCI self-service so you and your team can now focus on the two remaining steps of MCI development.
PEOPLE	In this step, the focus should lie entirely on engaging your user constituencies with small workshops, questionnaires, and possibly one-to-one interviews to improve your understanding of their needs and rationale regarding the new MCI system services you introduce. At this level, don't focus primarily on your need for more MCI topics, specific dialogues, and input; this will follow as a consequence and will be addressed in Levels 5 and 6.

Gardener tasks

<u>Director of MCI</u>

For the Director, the MCI operation is approaching a "going concern" with incremental development activities. Evolving from Plants to Flower Beds is viewed as expanding services offered with what now looks more like an in-house, advanced management consultancy. The key to success in this particular phase is interaction with user constituencies. One key suggested activity is to gather teams of archetypical decision-makers into "mini-workshops" to analyze and document their more personal needs, developing dashboards accordingly. Invite the decision-makers to use the dashboards as soon as possible afterward to keep pace.

Information specialist

As noted within the I component of the ITP, source selection work is changing in character and now becoming more of an ongoing source analysis and management task. Sources need constant evaluation and an ability to prepare for change, but overall, the operation is set. It is, therefore, an ongoing responsibility of the source specialist to maintain quality and economics in the source mix deployed. This also means he or she tends to, more so than in earlier levels, join forces with analysts to gain further insight about specific needs and share expertise for varied ongoing analytics projects.

Technology specialist

If the IT specialist enjoyed a momentary respite while evolving from Sprouts to Plants, it is now time to step up activity once again. Focus on the T components of ITP, implementing as many as possible during this development phase. In particular, ensure all system users acquaint themselves with, and start using, your MCI system's mobile interface, most notably sales reps using MCI battle cards

Analysts

To an extent, it is now time for analysts to revisit the initial mapping of models and procedures and, in turn, develop a standardized analytics framework that will form the foundation for future levels of development. For the Flower Beds level, ensure decision markers firmly define and evaluate the models. Specifically:

- Develop profiles/templates for your most common analysis targets such as companies, products, and markets. Recognizability and comparability are keys to success.

- Add specific target profiles such as battle cards for sales reps.

- Introduce structured benchmarking as a holistic tool for strategy and decision-making.

Decision-makers

In this development phase, decision-makers have one solitary task: continuously put analysis models to the test. This is an iterative procedure that must be rapid to engage and secure momentum.

Burgeoning: Evolving to Level 5—The Shrubberies

The vision

You are beginning to see the tendencies of a growing botanic garden.

For example, rhododendron shrubs provide healthy shadowing for both sensitive flower beds and visitors to the garden. Likewise, MCI serves as a true insights engine for the entire organization. The need for MCI is now even more demand-driven, and you no longer need to market your MCI platform.

Decision-makers want to engage, and you provide them with the means to do so. With distributed analytics and widespread usage of online as well as mobile tools provided through the MCI IT platform, the organization has set its path towards true self-serviced MCI insights for business processes. The MCI team is still proactively developing new capabilities yet also adding more long-term activities for ongoing MCI support to established company processes.

Key matters

By now, it is highly likely you boast a rather large group of "Observers," as we called them in the afore-mentioned Plants level. Observers are a committed group of colleagues who enjoy engaging in MCI inner communications and dialogue, providing your team with invaluable information and insights for your analysis. It is also likely that you and your team now have experience with different analysis tools, in-system or "offline," but more so on an ad-hoc basis. Encouraging your shrubberies to bloom is all about enabling a much more structured analysis, providing not only yourselves but also your Observers with systems-supported analysis tools to foster engagement and prepare for harvesting in Level 6 (but we will come back to that). Nurturing your garden from beautiful Flower Beds to hosting magnificent Shrubberies means you must:

- Spread analysis chart and tool usage, allowing users to visualize trends and patterns in your information

- Apply more structured Artificial Intelligence and Machine Learning-based tools to help you (e.g., discover, structure, cluster, recommend, translate, summarize information)

- Use APIs and connectors to seamlessly connect to third-party systems so users can access intelligence from their desired application
- Track system usage with metrics of your choice

For this development, we strongly recommend you revisit the chapter on taxonomies (Chapter 5) and, if you have not already done so, familiarize yourself with Chapter 8 content on Artificial Intelligence.

Information, Technology, People (ITP)

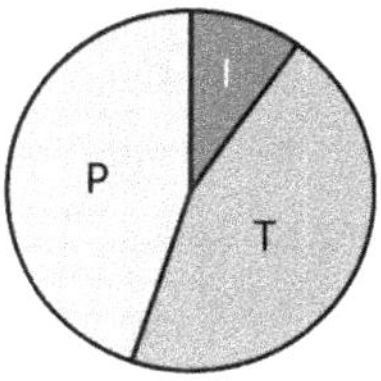

Share of work in the Burgeoning phase - the largest share of the work is in Technology and People.

INFORMATION	As in Level 4, you are now all set with the information at hand. Keep in mind that for each user group or analysis scope expansion, always revisit sourcing specifications to secure relevant system input. Keep doing what was initiated in Phase 4.
TECHNOLOGY	If Level 4 focused on expanding usage and information flows, this level is about significantly deepening the system and organization's analytics capabilities. For the former, execute the following: • Introduce analytics tools on a wider basis

- Discover trends supported by Machine Learning
- Integrate your system with other systems via APIs

These are described in further detail below.

Introduce analytics tools on a wider basis

Any MCI system today should feature a variety of tools for analysis and visualization, such as heatmap matrices, time graphs, word clouds, pie charts, bar charts, and clusters imaging. It is all a matter of visualizing structures within otherwise uninterpretable volumes of unstructured information. Whichever system at hand, make sure to familiarize yourself in detail with those tools and work with your MCI team to decide how these tools best support your analysis models agreed upon during Phase 4. Next, open up visualization functionality for your Observers and let them leverage the system power to become an even more valuable part of your MCI input.

Discover trends supported by Machine Learning

After you begin using the system tools for analysis, further development ensues. Either you have in-system capabilities for Machine Learning that you can support with trend analysis, artificially created topics, and advanced algorithm deployment, or you can use third-party tools. The key thing is to keep adding visualization and analysis support to the user interface for your MCI teams and Observers. The more you can inspire strategic considerations and insights, the better your organization will develop.

	Integrate your system with other systems via APIs In Phase 3, we already introduced the connection of your MCI system to internal sources such as common drives, MS Share Point, etc. Now is the time to bring your MCI data back to other systems. By way of APIs, employ BI tools such as Tableau or Power BI, feed insights into other intranet systems, or share your MCI data and insights with sales reps through their CRM interface. Most representations will include visualizations and raw news feeds to make it easier for users to consume information.
PEOPLE	We are now on our way to Level 5, and hitherto, it was only during Phase Three that we considered the People component as its own focus. It is thus time to step this up in preparation for the final Phase Six development. The key in this fifth development phase is to begin to engage your user constituencies in dialogue beyond output consumption. In this development, focus on: • Tracking usage to learn about organizational challenges • Supporting analyst workflow throughout the organization Tracking usage to learn about organizational challenges A key feature of any central productivity or analysis system must be the ability to track user behavior. Your MCI system now includes the entire MCI team, your Observers and a wide and growing range of decision-makers. Each provides the MCI team with log data about searches, favorite topics, alert usage, and much more, supporting the team in refining the MCI experience for all members of the organization.

You have the data—use it and enable faster, more qualitative decisions than would otherwise be the case.

<u>Supporting analyst workflow throughout the organization</u>
Finally, by now, it is likely that your MCI team has grown and consists of members who have never met all of their peers. To prepare for the next step in your development, document all templates, analysis models, and profiles. These instructions will allow new members to quickly adapt to the analysis workflow with a consensus on how to approach analytical challenges.

Gardener tasks

Director of MCI

Evolving from Flower Beds to Shrubberies is a rather natural progression wherein all was set to move in this direction after Level 3. The Director's key task is to continue to manage the team and quality of MCI processes already in place. However, this development phase includes ensuring all MCI procedures are well documented for "final MCI team expansion" in preparation for Harvesting and Blooming your Garden of Intelligence.

Information specialist

Continue as set out in Level 4.

Technology specialist

For the IT specialist, this is also an active phase of development. Focus on the aspects above. Again, your tool should already be prepared for the future, with new services and configurations added as well:

- Review your MCI tool's ability to visualize system content, mapping, and ability to support your agreed analysis models
- Open up analysis features to all Observers, providing usage instructions
- Take the first steps to embed machine-learning capabilities into your analysis environment, embarking on a MCI continuous improvement track that will evolve over time
- Connect to other internal systems via API and enable intranets, BI systems, and CRM to draw on content and insights that reside in the MCI system
- Initiate user behavior tracking and continuously refine system user needs, compliance and value

Analysts

Work closely with the IT specialist and now:

- Implement and "systemize" the results of Phase 4 development into the MCI platform for wide organization usage
- Make sure to document use-case instructions for all modules and procedures implemented
- Be prepared to undertake analysis training sessions/workshops for those who request them

Decision-makers

As with the source specialist, the decision-maker's role is by now set. Continue to put analysis models and tools to the test and support analysts as they seek to work in accordance with actual business needs.

Harvesting: Evolving to Level 6—The Blooming Garden

The vision

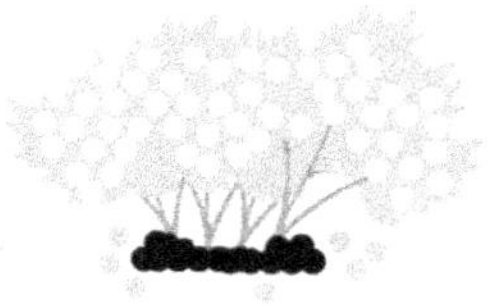

Time to declare success! Your garden is in full bloom.

Harvesting fruit, flowers, and herbs are ongoing activities while visitors enjoy and are amazed by the beauty and rigor of the garden design. An Intelligent Community is here! MCI is now embedded in the regular workings of the organization.

What was once a central MCI development and service team has evolved into a tool-and-process-providing operation, enabling the entire organization to optimize insights management for ongoing business. MCI has reached what can be considered its ultimate goal.

Key matters

So far, you built an MCI operation that masters the content base of your industry, analysis is conducted in a structured, recurrent way, and decision-makers can trust that information and insights provided are valid, thoughtful, and valuable. All in all, your organization's MCI has a real and appreciated impact on business results. The final development towards the Blooming Garden level is to significantly expand the analyst and decision-maker network into an Intelligent Community. Harvesting the beautiful, fully grown, fruit-bearing creation you envisioned means you will:

- Establish well-known and common communication processes that are transparent in your platform
- Engage management and all employees in sharing MCI and expertise
- Use Augmented Intelligence and AI-based tools to increase user capabilities, removing the need to allocate time and energy for repetitive tasks that can be automated
- Develop a dedicated Intelligent Community that can respond quickly and creatively to urgent intelligence topics. For this particular item, see Chapter 9. It is time-consuming, but the reward is worth it.

At the end of this development phase, you have made MCI a natural part of everyone's role, from top to bottom. Everyone continuously contributes and learns from the business environment, and MCI is a top agenda item at all important strategic gatherings, including board meetings.

Herein follows our final guidance and advice for your garden's fulfillment.

Information, Technology, People (ITP)

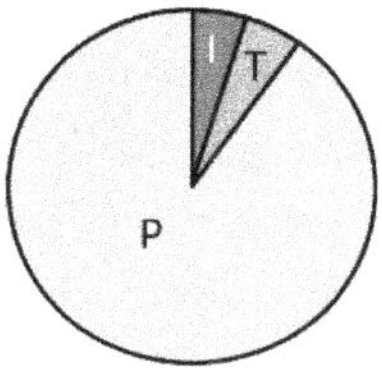

Share of work in the Harvesting phase - the largest share of the work is in People

INFORMATION	As in the two preceding phases, you are now all set with your information/content strategy. Just keep in mind to update sources according to newly identified needs.
TECHNOLOGY	Although some actions described under People in this chapter may require minimal fine-tuning within your MCI platform, it is all about people, people, and again…people. Therefore, this level will mimic actions taken in the previous two: namely, concluding that you have achieved your goal and must now focus on supporting your people's engagement ambitions.
PEOPLE	Now is the time to truly embed CI into the everyday operation of the entire company. The following three actions are the first to implement. Follow up with details in Chapters 9 and 10 to fulfill the Blooming Garden of Intelligence: • Enable sharing and collaboration • Promote expertise location

- Monitor evolving intelligence matters throughout the organization

Enable sharing and collaboration

You have already started to engage all employees as Observers, and by provoking responses, you initiated a "MCI dialog." Now is the time to significantly enlarge your team of MCI analysts so a "part-time analyst" exists in every corner of the organization. Find and engage these part-time analysts and provide them with tools to draw on the collective knowledge and wisdom of the entire organization. MCI will no longer serve as an "external" advisory function but rather a natural, integrated part of every decision. We call this an *Intelligent Community* (see Chapter 9). This network of part-time analysts is not formally part of the MCI team but use the MCI organization for their own benefit. However, to enable such collaborative models, the MCI team must train and engage these part-time analysts in MCI models and procedures to secure a "common MCI language" among all involved.

Promote expertise location

To draw on the organization's knowledge base, it is often most natural to turn to similar analysts in other parts of the organization. As a local analyst, you need support, and in other situations, will bring your insights to someone else in the global community of MCI analysts. Also, the fact that both parties are trained in the same manner will make knowledge sharing more efficient.

Beyond similar analysts, there are often specialized

experts, such as in product development, finance, and IP/legal/patent. They are typically only engaged in MCI on an ad-hoc basis, but it can add significant value with their deeper knowledge and expertise. From a MCI operations perspective, the team must promote functions for, and incentives to participate in, expertise networks and location.

Monitor the growth of MCI

Now that your garden is bearing fruit, any gardener will tell you that all organisms must be properly cared for—an Intelligent Community is no exception. Unless your garden is constantly nurtured, it can quickly stop growing or even start decaying. To prioritize your scarce resources, it is advisable to nurture where it is most needed and unearth those less well-growing parts of your MCI garden and develop a structured monitoring model to track development and growth. Ensure the MCI team fully engages in local MCI operations as support. That will also significantly strengthen the central team's ability to support company management with direct insight into local business challenges.

Gardener tasks

Director of MCI

It would be fair to say that by far, the two most demanding development phases for the Director exist from Level 1 to Level 2 and now from Level 5 to Level 6. Fully utilizing the team, it is now time to evolve per the P component of ITP. Concrete activities include:

- Bringing the best company strategists and your MCI team to a series of workshops to decide on a "final" and common MCI analysis framework—key questions to tackle include the best methods, jargon, and ways to communicate

- Designing a training program for the forthcoming Intelligent Community members, your local MCI analysts

- Ensuring you have support from company management to engage local resources who are not within your line or project management mandate

- Thoroughly building your incentive argument basis towards your forthcoming expert network and what's in it for them

- Hand selecting your first batch of local MCI analysts and, through training, coaching, and nurturing, building your Intelligent Community from there

Information specialist

Yes, we know you know—but for consistency's sake, allow us to discuss all gardener roles in all sections. Just keep doing what you now excel at and partake in all MCI team development activities under the guidance of the Director, as listed above.

Technology specialist

As with the information specialist, following the two preceding levels, you are now back in maintenance mode. Having said that, one imperative task is to take an active part in the P developments by, whenever called for, upgrading the MCI system configuration to cater to any new working models and procedures.

Analysts

This is the stage when the current group of analysts truly should do their best to clone themselves. Two key activities are therefore to:

- Develop a "handbook/manual" that describes all methods and jargon
- Support the Director in developing an organization-wide training program for local analysts on their way into the Intelligent MCI Community

Decision-makers

Decision-makers now have two foci. Continue as is from Phase 5 and showcase your work for any other business teams that have not yet fully embraced your MCI working models. If the analysts' job is to clone themselves within the MCI community, decision-makers should do the same in their respective user constituencies and also actively enable and promote a spill-over effect into similar teams throughout the organization.

How much time will it take?

How long time does it take to reach each level? How many hours of work are required? Variables that impact answers to these questions are as numerous as they are unforeseen. The time it takes will depend on the organization's size and scope. Overall, the biggest time factor is the organization's preparedness and company culture. Ideal levels of preparation and *senior* executive management support will decrease the number of hours needed to navigate diplomatic and not-yet-invented obstacles. The most unpredictable phases, duration wise, are the first and last.

Generally speaking, we find that once approval is obtained to create a garden, the first steps can be executed, and you will reap benefits relatively quickly. Upon reaching the final steps, you will find it becomes more of an ongoing, continuous effort.

Key takeaways

Summarizing the key takeaways of this chapter:

- The six different levels and corresponding development phases for your blooming Garden of Intelligence are described and explained in terms of the vision, key matters, ITP and gardeners tasks

- Each phase requires different focus on the ITP components:

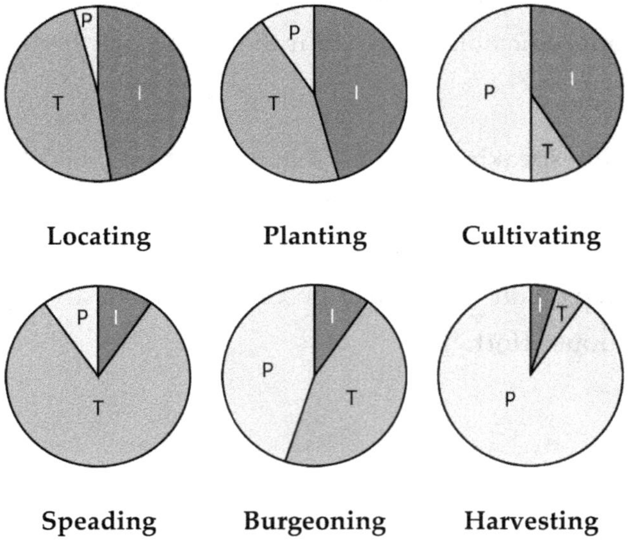

Part III

Digging Deeper

The third part provides more in-depth guidance into **how** to work with some key capability components that are essential for the buildup of Market & Competitive Intelligence, namely Information, Technology and People. Chapters 5 and 6 are about Information, Chapters 7 and 8 covers Technology, and Chapters 9 and 10 deal with the People capability.

CHAPTER 5

Navigating Information in a Structured Way

Finding information is often referred to as a rather simple task, and that is seemingly true. This process takes seconds these days, but is it the right information? Is it relevant? Is the source credible? Was it found in time to support the reason for the search in the first place? The truth is that when adding these criteria to the activity of finding information, it turns out to be a very complex task indeed.

This chapter outlines these challenges in more detail. It describes how to develop pre-set structures and algorithms to support information finding and aggregation given a particular organization's operations and need for insights. Structured use of the unstructured is a must in today's information environment.

The Challenge—Three Deep Jungles of Information

Jungles of information

Let's start from the beginning and identify what makes it so hard to find what you are looking for. We call this the "three deep jungles of information":

1. The Jungle of Overload
2. The Jungle of Storage
3. The Jungle of Retrieval

1. *The Jungle of Overload*

According to IDC, the volume of digital data will grow by 40% to 50% per year in the foreseeable future. As a consequence, the world's information is doubling every second year. For organizations, this means making quick and well-grounded business decisions are becoming increasingly difficult. It is certainly no longer possible for an individual to manually sift through the amount of information available, which in turn also renders it impossible to manually ensure all relevant information is at hand to make the best decision.

2. *The Jungle of Storage*

The approach of storing information, documents, and files in folder structures predates computers by at least 2,000 years. The Great Library of Alexandria in Egypt is the first known institution to use a structured and labeled system to store documents. Despite its long history, this practice has a great limitation—a document can only be stored in one place. How many documents written today feature only a single topic? Where should a document containing information about a particular company, product, technology, and market be stored? In the folder for Organization A or B, the folder for Product 1, 2, 3 or 4, or….? No doubt, every reader of this book recognizes this situation. Most would confess to having a difficult time making such decisions, even using their own devices. Bringing that challenge to the "shared network drives" many organizations use often results in an unmanageable mess of information stored according to individual perspectives on choosing the "one best place" for their documents. Everyone has their own way of categorizing things, which makes it hard for others to find.

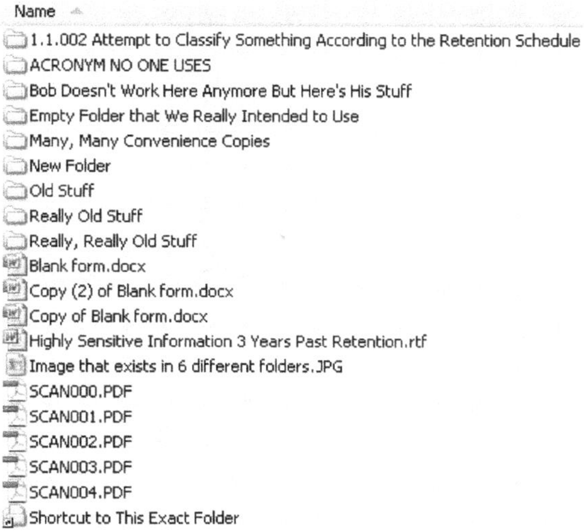

Messy information storage is not uncommon.

3. *The Jungle of Retrieval*

The two challenges described above result in the third and most costly challenge of them all—the inability of individual decision-makers to retrieve the information they need. Due to the volume of information, it is impossible to assess the relevancy and accuracy of all information at hand. In combination with a failed model for storing information, the result is often *"decisions made in the dark."* If this challenge is not addressed, the costs associated with not having relevant information to feed decision-making are enormous. Highly competent individuals are expected to utilize the organization's proprietary information and use their knowledge to derive value within their job roles. It is nothing short of value destruction if they cannot access and use existing information due to lacking structures and support systems. The consequence is that pre-existing information very often must be reinvented over and over again.

The predominant situation is that there is far too much information to digest, it is badly stored and structured, and filtering systems, if they even exist, don't meet anyone's needs.

Structured information management and data governance

From an individual information user's perspective, the prevailing situation is that there is far too much information to digest, it is badly stored and structured, and filtering systems, if they even exist, don't meet anyone's needs—and worse, maintenance is a manual task. A new approach is needed!

One of the best tools to overcome the three "jungles" described above is simply a structure. A structured approach to information management and data governance makes the collection, analysis, and dissemination of information faster and more efficient.

Organizations must have a logical structure to index and access relevant business information, meaning a classification system that allows all information to be categorized with ***multiple topics***. Returning to the example above, the choice should not be either Organization A, Product 3, or Market 2—it should be all. A familiar analogy is tagging pictures on social media sites such as Facebook. It's not surprising for a picture to be tagged with multiple "topics" such as grandma, grandpa, sister, or best friend. The only difference in a business information context is that content is tagged with relevant business topics instead of relatives and friends.

Information is thereby obtained through multiple entry points, and as a result, organizing, navigating, and finding information is a structured, efficient process. As such, it is driven by future user needs rather than storage decisions made by producers.

Taxonomies—A widely used tool for classification

Taxonomies—how can such a powerful concept and tool for information management in general, and MCI in particular, attract so many varied opinions? We will come back to that, but with more than 25 years of practical experience in business taxonomies, spanning both MCI and Knowledge Management, we are confident to say this is one of the most powerful tools (if not the only tool) currently available to manage and make use and sense of the ever-growing set of unstructured information.

> *Without a taxonomy, you will remain lost in a no man's land of information overload.*

Taxonomies help people and organizations apply structure to vast amounts of otherwise unstructured information. They support organizations that must make fast and well-informed business decisions and overcome one of the largest problems facing companies today: "information fog." Without a taxonomy, you will remain lost in a no man's land of information overload.

Fundamentally, a **taxonomy serves as a classification system—a standardized, controlled set of topics, terms, and phrases.** Vocabulary.com has an explanation much to the point: "Taxonomy is a word used mainly in biology to talk about classifying living organisms, organizing them according to their similarities. If you've ever seen a chart with animals divided into *species*, *genus*, and *family*, you know what scientific taxonomy is. The word comes very straightforwardly from Greek words for "arrangement" — *taxis* — and "method" — *nomia*. So any special method for arranging or organizing things can be called *taxonomy*."

A business taxonomy should enable procedures to minimize time spent looking for required information and ensure all relevant information is taken into consideration.

Although taxonomies have historically held a large role in biology, such as for plant and animal classification, they are also widely used in library sciences, wherein books are classified according to a structure that makes them easy to find. Taxonomies in a business context serve a similar purpose, but in this case, are used to categorize information to facilitate storage and retrieval as information primarily supports decision-making. A business taxonomy should enable procedures to minimize time spent looking for required information and ensure all relevant information is taken into consideration.

It is fair to say that a folder structure is one possible representation of a taxonomy. Still, in the context of today's business needs, we have already discarded that as an insufficient approach. Rather, we design a taxonomy for "tagging."

In the illustration below, a very simple "taxonomy" is outlined in the form of a traditional folder structure. It is hierarchical with an intuitive structure—under the root topic "Countries," you will find countries, and so forth, in other business dimensions. A bad taxonomy is not intuitive on each level, meaning that it's difficult to anticipate what lies ahead if the view is expanded when one level is viewed. Other examples of failed taxonomies are those in which similar, or worse, *identical,* topics appear in different structure branches or those that include assessments of specific topics by sorting companies into groups like customers, suppliers, and competitors. A customer for one part of an organization can be a supplier for others, and the same goes for a competitor who is perhaps a customer elsewhere. Even structuring according to regions, as illustrated below, is debatable. On numerous occasions, we meet customers from a regional organization that does not match the typical geographical representation, in turn injecting confusion into the taxonomy (a big no-no):

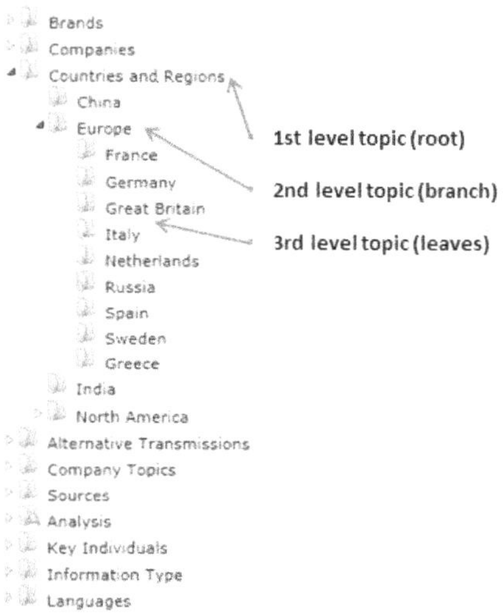

A taxonomy has roots, branches, and leaves.

In fact, this particular illustration is a few years old and contains more than one irregularity we would not accept as "taxonomists." Try to decipher what these are—we will provide an answer later on in the chapter and elaborate on traps like these in the section on developing a context-based taxonomy.

For now, back to the acclaimed problems and arguments regarding the limited value of taxonomies. Many business gurus, mainly in the field of knowledge management, have always claimed that taxonomies do not help address the information management challenges at hand. We strongly disagree and believe this group of people, no matter how many brilliant business development ideas they've contributed, in this case missed the fact that varied types of taxonomies exist. What they are referring to are so-called content-driven taxonomies, with which we agree wholeheartedly. However, it is not what *currently* exists that matters—it is what *should* exist, which is modeled in context-driven taxonomies. Hence, it is essential to clarify the difference between content-driven and context-driven taxonomies.

Content-driven taxonomies

Traditionally, we use taxonomies to classify and codify information that is already at hand. Think about a traditional library. There are elaborate systems to know exactly what shelf to place a book about British countryside cooking during the Victorian era. However, we can apply this system only to *existing* books, not those still forming in the minds of their authors. Unfortunately, the same concept sometimes applies to corporate taxonomies built to answer the question, "What information do we have?" If we develop corporate taxonomies without concepts such as customers, competitors, partners, or other external factors in mind, they become very inward-looking. This misses the point of even having a taxonomy, especially from a MCI perspective.

Context-driven taxonomies

On the other hand, a context, or needs-driven, taxonomy should answer the question, "What information *should* we have?" A taxonomy used for MCI purposes should reflect the industry and highlight intelligence important for the organization's future growth and success. This means that if a topic is left empty, this is not necessarily a bad thing. For example, there may be a gap or blind spot in understanding the business environment that is knowingly, by the topic's sheer emptiness, identified.

> *A taxonomy used for MCI purposes should reflect the industry and highlight intelligence that is important for the organization's future growth and success.*

Consequently, the procedures used to develop a needs-driven taxonomy differ significantly from those employed to develop a content-driven taxonomy. The former type is key for both MCI and Knowledge Management, as market changes and the need to adapt to the business environment fundamentally drive both.

Developing a context-driven taxonomy

Developing a context-driven taxonomy involves teamwork and a series of workshops with varied stakeholders in the user community. Using data governance terminology, the data steward, alongside architects and operations modelers, undertakes this process to specify business glossary standards for information assets. In our MCI terminology, we prefer to discuss the business dimensions of the taxonomy in development, but for those readers with data governance perspectives, this is where our roads very much meet.

In stark contrast to "traditional" taxonomies that "classify" information using a single label and folder (or bookshelf), classifying information with *multiple* topics generates vast opportunities for organizations managing large quantities of information. The method used to create a corporate taxonomy thus involves assessing the need for varied topics about decision mandates throughout the organization. Most individual knowledge needs within an organization are related to one or more of the following tags or topics:

- An organization (e.g., customer, competitor, or supplier)
- An organization topic (e.g., finance, strategy, organization, or pricing)
- A product/service (e.g., any product from the product catalog or competing products)

- A product character (e.g., technical specs, pricing, or market penetration)
- A country
- A country topic (e.g., economics, security, or industry regulations)

In addition to the topic areas listed above, there are industry-specific topics such as regulations and government matters. Still, as a basic taxonomy, the above is found in almost every company.

While this structure may seem simple enough to model, the many hours we've dedicated to this task within company modeling workshops prove otherwise. The complexity primarily lies in two perspectives:

- Varied individuals seek to embed different "assessments" within the topic structure, whereas none should exist—it can be difficult for a team lacking taxonomy development experience to see the traps.
- Many find it tremendously complex to adopt an outside-in (rather than inside-out) development mode. By that, we mean, for example, a taxonomy that even touches the organizational structure is doomed to fail as a context-driven taxonomy.

Another complexity is to ensure process and assessment-based parts of the taxonomy are truly orthogonal to its business dimensions—indeed, a third trap that many encounter in their first taxonomy development experience. We will revisit the process and assessment-based parts in the next section.

Workshopping the business dimensions must involve internal industry experts who can illustrate the organization's entire business environment and sufficiently condense that into a manageable information model. The most important trap to avoid is using "internal lingo" rather than industry-standard labels. Then, perform a sanity check to eliminate ambiguities, for instance, is this really a product or rather a technology? In many situations, this requires a significant time investment.

Let's revisit the folder-represented taxonomy above and discuss associated ambiguities/traps. Why is it a flawed example?

- Brands versus companies—although it is correct these are different, but are all taxonomy users aware of the difference between the brand BMW and the company Bayerische Motoren Werke AG? There is a risk of confusion regarding the relationship between company and brand names. Think this through.

- Alternative transmissions—a root topic on the same level as "Companies," when it should intuitively fall under a root labeled "Technologies," or the like. This is an architectural mistake that severely undermines the structure's intuitive nature.

- China, Europe, and India exist on the same level under Countries and Regions. Are China and India not part of the region "Asia" in that case?

- Europe? Do we mean Europe or EU? Classic confusion in this structure is suddenly amplified as Great Britain is no longer part of the EU but is part of Europe.

These are but four examples of mistakes right from the get go at Levels 1 and 2 in a very(!) simple taxonomy structure. Expanding that to hundreds (or thousands) of topics and mistakes like these are fatal to overall usability.

Using this type of thinking, assign all relevant topics to a particular piece of information. As a result, the data has multiple entry points that allow different users to find the same information, independent of individual perspectives.

When you create a taxonomy, assign each topic algorithms, keywords, search strings, and patterns as applicable, often using Boolean logic or Regular Expression pattern matching. This will enable the automated taxonomy to assign the right topics to each piece of information by scanning the content and allowing the taxonomy to perform the bulk filtration for you.

There are specific types of topics that are better suited for automated classification than others, which we will elaborate on further in the section on that topic.

Adding process and assessment classification to your taxonomy

In addition to the business dimensions of a taxonomy (which is normally by far the largest part), it should typically include two additional ones: work processes and analytical assessments.

As a MCI analyst, a significant portion of the work is packaging content into special reports, creating weekly targeted newsletters, and assessing information from varied analysis model perspectives, such as PEST, SWOT, Porter's Five Forces, and Porter's Four Corners.

Since you should implement a taxonomy in such a way that you can add and manage pre-tagged topics on any document, a time-saving exercise is to add a dimension to the taxonomy that reflects your work and analysis models. With that in place, the MCI analyst can use the business dimension topics to filter out relevant content and then swiftly add topics that reflect the analysis perspective and the intended information dissemination mode. Such a taxonomy dimension is typically designed as follows, but can, of course, cater to any other work model your particular company may favor:

- Analysis (PEST, SWOT, Porter's 5F) (with subtopics for each such as Strength)
- Output format (Brief, Alert, Weekly report, Monthly report, Quarterly report, Company report, Product report, Market report)
- Process (Potential, Draft, Selected, Final)

Core process topics, such as CRM/ERP systems, can be added to the process dimension to align MCI with the organization's development and delivery processes.

Also, the concept of Key Intelligence Topics (KITs) is often used in MCI operations for very specific focus questions at each point in time. Although KITs should definitely be part of a MCI platform taxonomy, they are but a subset of what the MCI platform should address.

With a taxonomy that matches the organization's business environment, strategy, and work models, the tedious task of gathering and compiling information is not only more bearable but a rather joyful exercise as results are visible immediately.

The battle between manual and automatic classification

Classifying information assets into taxonomy topics is done either automatically or manually. Both have their pros and cons. Some topic types are better suited for one, and others for its counterpart. Due to reasons that are difficult to understand, this is also a field wherein opinions are sometimes strong and very black or white. The best solution is typically a combination, but let's examine the matter in greater detail.

Manual classification is performed by editors or administrators who have the right to publish and edit documents/articles and manually add topics based on their individual judgment.

Automatic classification involves creating a set of algorithms for each taxonomy topic. Such fine-tuning is either manual or supported by Machine Learning. This type of classification is triggered by identifying keywords, phrases, and patterns within the content, then tagging it into applicable topics. Each topic is associated with an unlimited set of classification algorithms or rules. Chapter 8 further elaborates on the topics of ML and AI for classification automation.

The main difference between automatic and manual classification is that the former is objective while the latter is subjective. Two people seldom have the same opinion on metadata or topics.

The major benefit of automatic classification is that it allows organizations to sift through large amounts of information each day without requiring human resources, thus allowing individuals to spend more time analyzing and applying it. Consider reading an article to assess whether it impacts your business and if so, tag it per company taxonomy. As an individual, you can only read one article at a time. In a best-case scenario, know the entire taxonomy well enough to tag it properly (although even that is unusual). With automated classification, you can instead ensure topics themselves "read" all incoming content/documents simultaneously, and with almost identical "assessments," you personally decide whether to tag the article with a specific topic. The difference? The automated topic can read thousands of information assets in a fraction of the time it takes you to read but one. With an automated taxonomy, your document libraries will, despite the size and pace they grow, always possess the labeling needed for your decision-makers to retrieve relevant information.

The benefit of manual classification, on the other hand, is that tagging in itself is an analysis (notably well-suited for more abstract topics such as Opportunity/Threat, Strategy, Positive/Negative). Still, people are usually unaware of what topics may interest a department other than their own. They also lack the time required to execute the exercise to its full extent, stifling its overall quality.

To fully conclude the arguments for and against manual versus automatic classification, the matter must be divided into three main categories:

- Business dimensions-based classification
- Assessment-based classification
- Process-based classification

For business dimensions (organizations, products, countries, regulators, etc.) automated classification wins by magnitudes. No subjectivity is needed or even desired, with only standard topics considered.

Assessment-based classification, on the other hand, is almost the opposite. Is this good or bad for us? Is this a strategy or operations matter? Few, if any, current algorithms can do more than merely suggest thoughts about the topic (apologies to all you overenthusiastic AI fans who cannot fathom its limitations), so it must simply be a human task. One example is if you manually add "company strategy" to a document tagged with a certain company. By seeing this topic tag, a user will automatically know this information is about company strategy. A complex process is required for auto-tagging to get it right at this level, but, again, it can support the analyst working with assessment-based tagging. The amount of information that benefits from this kind of classification is but a small fraction of the total, so it is significantly more manageable than manually classifying business dimensions.

Process-based classification falls somewhere in between. Most information assets ripe for this classification type are either internally originated data from CRM, ERP, or project systems. This volume is manageable in such cases, as with assessment classification, easily afforded relevant metadata from its source systems (auto classified) or external data that must be classified per varied analytical processes such as SWOT, P5F, or the like.

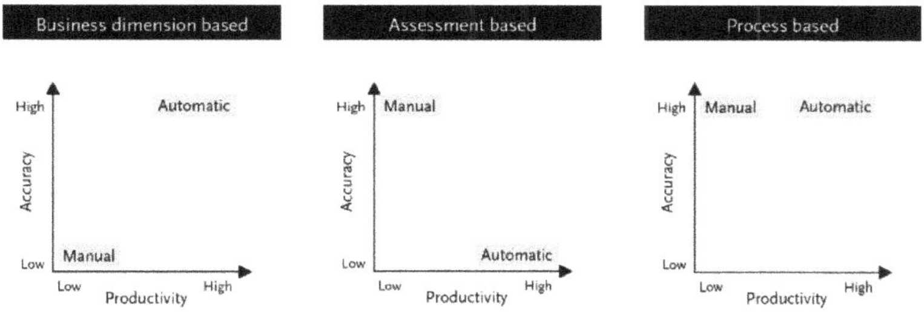

Pros and cons of automatic versus manual classification.

Benefits of classification

Content classification helps your organization address the ever-increasing amount of information by speeding up and improving qualitative searches. A taxonomy that automatically helps tag information provides organizations with a better overview of their business landscape and frees up time for analysis. It also offers a better way to share information and knowledge within an organization, ensuring no wasted resources and leveraging existing capabilities.

By browsing information tagged with specific topics, one can instantaneously narrow down the scope of search and filtering. Furthermore, when adding topics to a query, search results gain relevancy, and time is saved by searching a smaller amount of information rather than a long list of documents. In addition to these benefits, there are also less obvious ones gained from the actual process of creating a taxonomy optimized for business. For example:

- Unifying corporate language and terminology
- Creating a shared map of intelligence needs for the organization

If the taxonomy reflects the organization's intelligence needs, it clearly visualizes what is important to know for the whole organization. As a result, people will use the same topic names in regular internal communication. Another often-overlooked benefit of a good taxonomy is that it encourages more people to become MCI explorers by creating a shared and updated business landscape map, thus improving strategic communication within your organization.

A visual example

What does a taxonomy look like in the "real world"? It can be graphically represented in many ways, but the following illustration is an excellent example of a visually powerful representation for search and filtering purposes:

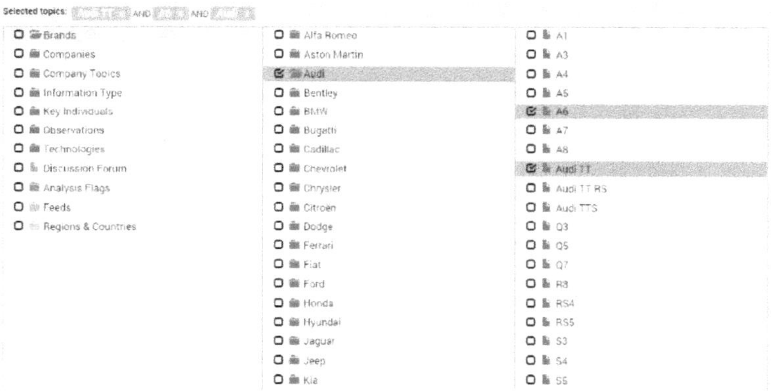

Example of horizontal taxonomy wherein the first column contains root topics, followed by second and third-layer subtopics.

By combining topics from varied roots and subtopics, one can apply a highly efficient filter. Typical examples in the taxonomy illustrated above could combine brand, technology, and patents—or a brand, a market, and marketing strategy. In cases like these, the filter reduces thousands of documents to only those that match selected combined topics, gaining relevance in seconds!

Key takeaways

Summarizing the key takeaways of this chapter:

- MCI taxonomies are based on business context and decision areas, not the content at hand.
- MCI taxonomies are dynamic and adaptable to change.
- MCI taxonomies allow each piece of information to be classified into multiple topics, not just one.
- MCI taxonomies avoid duplicate topics (think in terms of "tags").
- MCI taxonomies are simple and easy to use—for everyone!

CHAPTER 6

Selecting Relevant Information Sources

So far, we have argued that a structured use of the unstructured is needed to make sense of all information at hand. The immediate next question is which information (sources to use) that exactly is. Without relevant content, a MCI system remains empty and useless.

By source, we mean all places where you can find information, including:

- open sources on the internet (e.g., Google, company websites)
- paid sources (e.g., major news sites such as FT.com and the Economist, but also specialized sources such as industry and financial analysts)
- internal data residing on an organization's intranet or the like
- employees and researchers proactively providing information

"Can't you just Google it?" some ask. Sure, but remember Google is not a search engine for business, but rather an online media platform that loads search results based on a user's private browsing behavior. It is driven by paid ads and content popularity, not relevance. Google will not encompass all sources needed for insights. And last but not least are security concerns as you leave your digital footprints behind. As such, Google is simply not the tool for analysts searching for a specific needle in any given haystack.

Deploying a vague sourcing strategy can prove tremendously costly. This chapter discusses the varied sources available, their pros and cons, and how to best build a source portfolio, step by step, that meets the needs but also boasts an acceptable "price/performance ratio."

Let's start by imagining your sources as the "huge haystack of unstructured data." Next, pretend you must quickly search through it to locate the "golden information needles" urgently required. Finally, picture the haystack as not only growing in size every time you see it but also new haystacks that start to appear in other places. No doubt, this makes it harder and harder to find the needles, right?

Yet, this is the information world we live in today. The key sourcing challenge is obviously how to address the huge volume of information flows. Getting this part right is so important to grow a Garden of Intelligence that we strongly suggest separating the information source selection from technology tools to ensure the former is truly independent.

In other words, you should, at any point, be able to easily adjust your mix of sources without the need to overhaul your entire IT platform.

You should, at any point, be able to easily adjust your mix of sources without the need to overhaul your entire IT platform.

This chapter addresses a very straightforward question: **What types of sources are there and how can you best use them?** It is, of course, beyond the scope of an overview like this to provide holistic, detailed coverage of all available sources for all industries. Rather, we aim to offer:

- a structural model for how to segment your particular set of sources
- a model for source mix planning with regards to available budgets

Segmenting information sources

Gathering information is not a challenge these days, as it is ubiquitous in most industries. Instead, the challenge is to gather ***relevant*** information. And believe it or not, not all relevant information is publicly available on the internet. To find the right information for *your* needs, varied sources are required.

Believe it or not, not all relevant information is publicly available on the internet.

Consciously selecting and managing sources is one way to narrow down the target information to a digestible volume of useful content. In other words, set out to shrink the haystack you're searching. To start, let's segment the entire source landscape into two very generic categories, with two subcategories each:

- External Sources
    - *Open sources* such as websites, news sources, and social media
    - *Commercial sources* such as analysis companies, market research, and news agencies
- Internal Sources
    - *Observers*, such as your employees/colleagues, partners, and

possibly suppliers and researchers throughout your organization value chains

- *Content* produced by your employees such as shared drives, SharePoint sites, CRM systems, and e-mail

Strangely enough, it is still not uncommon to address these two in different systems, which, of course, dilutes the ability to find significant patterns. The way one chooses to mix these sources significantly impacts output and required work volume/costs, so let's examine a brief overview of each category.

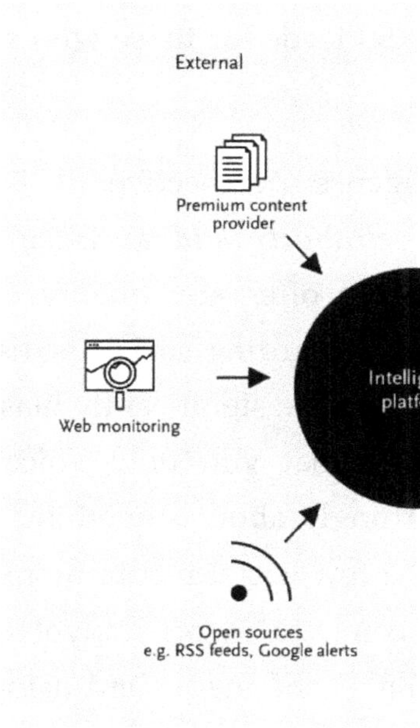

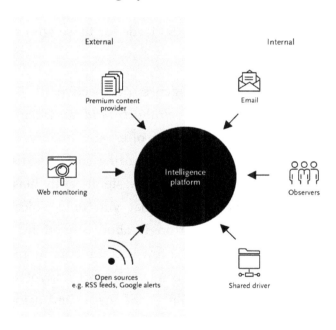

An Intelligence platform contains both external and internal sources

External sources—open

Open sources are publicly available and often provided free of charge. As a result, they have seen a never-ending increase in popularity over recent decades. "It's all free on the internet" is now a dogma that justifies an information overload situation that few companies can cope with.

Today, magazine e-mail and Google alerts, social media, and web spider services are examples of free or near-free information sources. RSS (Rich Site Summary) is a popular format to deliver evolving web content. Many news-related sites, weblogs, and other online publishers syndicate their content as RSS feeds for those who seek to consume it.

However, from an intelligence perspective, it is very important to consider the ***reliability and accuracy*** of the content. Open sources do not offer any quality control whatsoever for free content. Regarding social media, it is also apparent that most sources are significantly biased, as the typical web behavior is that you only voice your opinion if you feel very strongly about something (often mainly negative views). The few social media monitoring strategies that really seem to work involve the organization itself "controlling" the media and using it to probe large user or customer groups.

Is this to say that open-source content should not be used at all? No, definitely not, but be sure to make selections carefully to avoid drowning in a tsunami of irrelevant internet links.

External sources—commercial

Quality before Quantity. That is, only retrieve the most relevant and trusted external sources is probably the best way to summarize the argument for commercial sources. Be prepared to pay for high-quality content, but know it will be worth it in the end. The return on investment is usually obvious to companies that embark on this route. Use technology to automatically filter and categorize the selected sources according to your view of the world.

Be prepared to pay for high-quality content, but know it will be worth it in the end.

The commercial sources market is huge, and it is thereby helpful to further segment it to aid manageability. Specifically, it can be divided into four unique vendor categories:

- *Aggregators of free (open source) content*: These are typically web crawlers, so-called "agents," Google services, etc. Costs range from almost nothing to big-ticket prices, depending on the level of services available to support customers in both content selection and usage.

- *Aggregators of commercial content*: Major examples in this category are Dow Jones/Factiva, Bloomberg, Refinitiv, FactSet, Reuters, and LexisNexis. The vast majority of their sources are professional news bureaus or other copyright-protected content providers.
- *Pure originators of content*: These are companies who provide subscription-based information services but with customer-specific delivery limits. One premium example is the Economist Intelligence Unit (EIU).
- *Research and consulting companies*: These range from small niche boutique analysts, to market researchers, to major consulting firms, and selections are particularly needs-specific. This is also typically where quality service for primary research intelligence is found.

It is important to realize different vendor categories boast markedly different business models and that understanding them will help the sourcing manager craft an optimal mix of sources within a reasonable budget. It is worth investigating this market for a specific industry and learning how to optimize a commercial source mix.

People are the eyes and ears of any company and yet rarely used for intelligence purposes.

Internal sources—observers and subject matter experts

People are the eyes and ears of any company and yet rarely used for intelligence purposes. It is truly distressing to see so many experts not properly utilized for MCI processes within their organizations simply due to a lack of supporting tools to involve them in analytical procedures. Still, with little effort any company can develop a wide, distributed network of sporadic collectors wherein all employees, and partners alike, are encouraged to participate. By doing this, the organization develops a tremendous capability to identify a wide range of market signals.

It's easy! Enable any employee to contribute via web forms, mobile forms, or directly by e-mail. Add to this a simple touch of gamification, and your employees will participate as part of the daily fun. The challenge with this source type is to keep it going. Feedback loops are needed, and a clear sense of quality control raises the "status" of being quoted and sought after for further information. Hence, this source is much more sensitive than others regarding the content's final destination once it is fed into the intelligence apparatus. See Chapter 9 for further discussion on challenges and ways forward for this topic.

People can take on two very distinct roles: first, as a source (labeled "observers") and then as subject matter experts. In the latter, such individuals are so invaluable to MCI that they help evaluate information relevance within their particular field of expertise in the analytical process better than anyone. As observers, however, people function more as triggers of dialog or originators of primary intelligence.

Primary sources should be considered the pinnacle of intelligence gathering, probing specific questions and syntheses identified by structured analysis of the vast amount of information available through secondary sources.

By far, the most underutilized and least leveraged source of all is your organization's internal information.

Internal sources—content

In most organizations, larger ones in particular, ***internal information*** is by far the most underutilized and least leveraged source of all. This is the only content (with the obvious exception of Observer input) that you know with 100% certainty is not in competitors' hands. Competing companies often possess the same external information, but it is the ability to draw the best conclusions concerning one's own company's strategy that selects the winner, a battle in which utilizing a mix of external and internal information is a major advantage over only relying on the former. Unfortunately, this source base is often ill-managed, and if no clear Knowledge Management initiative (or the like) exists within the organization, the intelligence apparatus is often left in the dark. Making use of a global organization's entire content base is a very challenging task unless approved internal tools can be used to do so. Concrete examples of internal sources include:

- Shared drives
- SharePoint/Teams sites
- CRM systems
- Structured/relational databases
- Exchange/e-mail

A challenge worth noting in today's corporate environments is that of cloud storage. Depending on how they are structured and which service providers are used, integration/connector setups can be cumbersome. However, a cloud environment with a thought-through data governance structure should not add more complexity to a task than a traditional share drive structure (and certainly less than the most common these days, a wild grown collection of disparate SharePoint stacks). These are matters for the following two chapters, though.

Creating the right source mix

Once you understand the different types of sources available, you must narrow that down and create the right source mix for your organization. The sources you select obviously have a huge impact on the result of your intelligence work, so tread carefully. They should reflect the needs of your particular organization. That is, which "needles" you're looking for in your haystack.

To help you do this, we recommend you employ the following information structure:

- Gather the information we know we need.
- Gather the information we do not yet know we need.
- Avoid all information we know we do not need.

So, what do we mean by "need?" In very broad terms, this can be specified as:

- Information supporting the current strategy
- Information challenging the current strategy

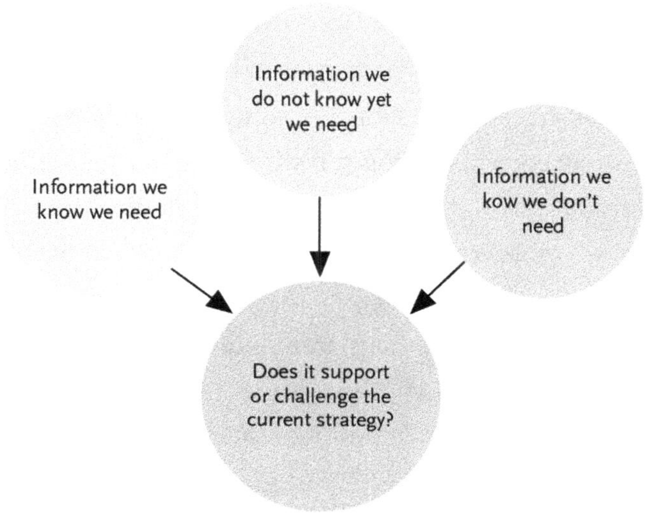

Segmenting sources

Structuring your information needs

Reviewing these statements, we quickly see that the "easy part" is gathering information we know we need about current strategy deployment needs, such as general market information, competitor watch, customer analysis, pricing support, and product benchmarks. This is the "classical" MCI scope to perform intelligence analysis to support company operations.

We consider information we do not know we need to challenge the current strategy on the other end of the scale. History shows that a failure to gather and act upon such information is a key reason why companies go out of business, so the importance cannot be underestimated. Yet, finding sources for this kind of content is perhaps the most difficult as corresponding questions are not yet defined. A preferred starting point are methodologies for "future analysis," as described in Chapter 10. They need not be as elaborate as therein suggested just for this purpose, but related thinking will help tremendously in mapping the unknown. Still, the key to success is to balance the types of sources with needs categories to enable a cost-efficient source selection.

With all segments in place, one can match the different source types with the different needs segments. A major challenge is to filter out unnecessary content. Remember that external commercial sources are usually easier to start with since you can pay them to deliver exactly what you need. Internal sources, such as your Observers, often have the most valuable information, but it can be difficult to motivate people to share what they have.

Continuously tuning your source mix

Voila! You now have your source mix well defined and are hence ready for the next steps, right? You have indeed taken a huge leap forward in terms of intelligence capabilities, but sources must be continuously monitored and tweaked in line with your business and market evolution. This is, however, not as complex as it might sound; it must merely be recognized.

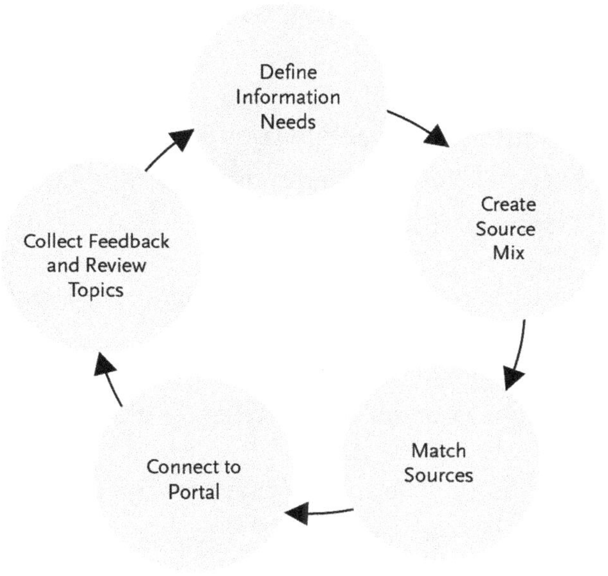

Revisit the taxonomy of topics and sources regularly, such as every quarter or at least once a year. The process is illustrated by this image.

Selecting sources for an enterprise intelligence operation is a complex and time-consuming task. It is, however, worth every minute as the typical outcome is a vastly better informed and insightful company.

Key takeaways

Summarizing the key takeaways of this chapter:

- Make sure to build a *mix* of all source types to avoid bias.
- Continuously evaluate your sources to ensure they keep providing both the right quantity and quality of information.
- Be prepared to pay for high-quality information.
- Consider separating content from technology tools to select your sources independently.
- Selecting relevant sources for an enterprise intelligence operation is a complex task but worth every minute invested in the process.

CHAPTER 7

How to Build a MCI Technology Platform[6]

By now, it should be evident that you need a technology tool that supports intelligence activity, both for production and delivery. The terms 'MCI portals,' 'Intelligence systems,' 'Insight engines,' 'MCI software' are heard everywhere, but what do they really mean? And why should you really care?

This chapter focuses on technology tools for MCI. The purpose is to clarify the concept of MCI software platforms, their range of functionalities, and the benefits an intelligence team should expect them to provide when sowing their Garden of Intelligence.

[6] Parts of this chapter are taken from "Introduction to Competitive Intelligence Portals" by Gabriel Anderbjörk & Jesper Martell. SCIP Competitive Intelligence Magazine, Volume 18, Number 3, July/September 2015.

What is a MCI technology platform?

The key purpose of a MCI platform is to provide a single access point to both external and internal sources for all producers and consumers of intelligence within your organization.

A MCI platform is a digital AI-assisted platform that automates intelligence work by:

- Collecting and classifying external and internal sources about the market/business environment
- Allowing users to not only glean news alerts, but serve themselves by searching/curating content
- Providing visualization features that enable users to analyze and discover new trends
- Delivering and sharing actionable insights using dashboards, alerts, templates, reports, and collaboration features

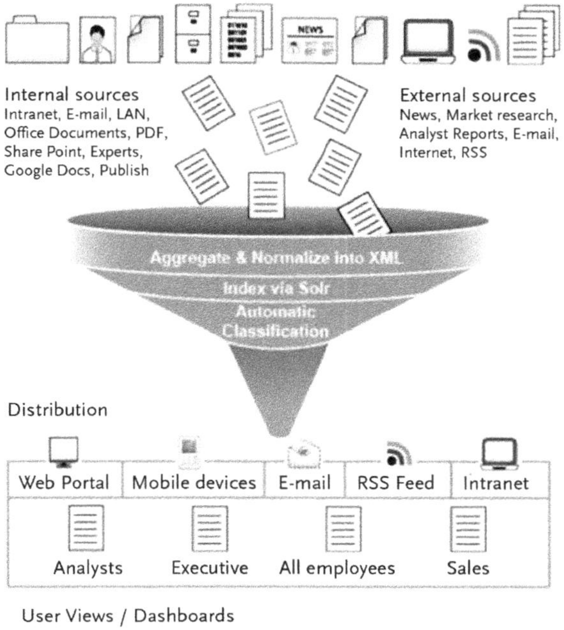

Example of MCI technology platform architecture

COLLECT

Input: Seamlessly unifies information from a broad spectrum of internal and external sources to paint a single picture of all enterprise information

PROCESS and ANALYZE

Engine: Automated data enrichment and advanced search technology add context and meaning to large volumes of unstructured content

DELIVER

Output: Provides a knowledge repository wherein users discover and share insights via user-friendly platforms, mobile devices, alerts, and other applications

An MCI platform collects, processes, analyses and delivers insights to relevant users.[7]

Do you really need a MCI platform?

MCI platforms are all about managing and visualizing information and the people who use it. The main challenge of MCI is no longer to *find* information but to *make sense* of the abundance available while filtering out seemingly small elements that might indicate a significant change or disruption ahead.

The job of an MCI professional is **not** to add to this volume of content but to deduce which information is relevant and find new sources—actually scale back information. Irrelevant data must be filtered out—often a difficult decision to make, but essential to avoid copious amounts of information. Then we draw insight from the remaining content. This is virtually impossible to do today without

---

[7] Source: Intelligence2day® by Comintelli.

technology support. So, yes! Some form of a MCI platform is needed to keep pace today. If your competitors have this and you don't, you have an immediate disadvantage in the marketplace.

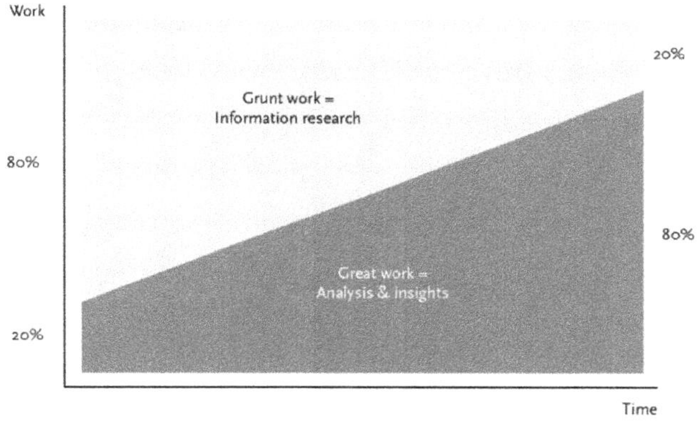

MCI tools allow you to do less GRUNT work (like searching and classifying information) and more GREAT work (like analyzing and creating insights).

A MCI platform has many advantages:

- It is not only a working tool for the entire MCI team but a service platform for all intelligence users.
- For the MCI team, a platform enables technology that automates the process and frees up time for analysis.
- A well-designed MCI platform supports intelligence work for both MCI producers and consumers.

- It helps inspire an intelligence culture by sharing important data and enabling communication between all platform users, intelligence consumers, and MCI professionals.
- It is one of the most tangible elements of MCI, and as such, is an excellent MCI marketing and communication tool.

Monitor and discover

Monitoring what you already know continuously is common sense and needed in all organizations. This includes tracking top competitors, customers, and your defined key intelligence topics. Monitoring information is an important foundation for MCI work, **but** it cannot serve as its only output. We wish to make a key point that a MCI platform is about more than simply monitoring web news and producing newsletters reflecting past events.

A MCI platform is about more than simply monitoring web news and producing newsletters reflecting past events.

In addition to monitoring information, MCI platforms should have the capability to support MCI to **discover** and create *new* insights. Two areas support discovery:

- First, MCI platforms should support a process or workflow for users who analyze information, draw conclusions and generate insights—in other words, putting information into context and *adding value* to it. This includes, for example, the ability to collaborate on creating reports, easily filtering and selecting the most relevant pieces of information that are approved and validated.

- Second, MCI platforms should help visualize trends and patterns within the flow of information—in other words, detect early signals for things not yet in existence. This includes, for example, AI-based clustering, word clouds, heat maps, trend graphs, and other visual analytics tools.

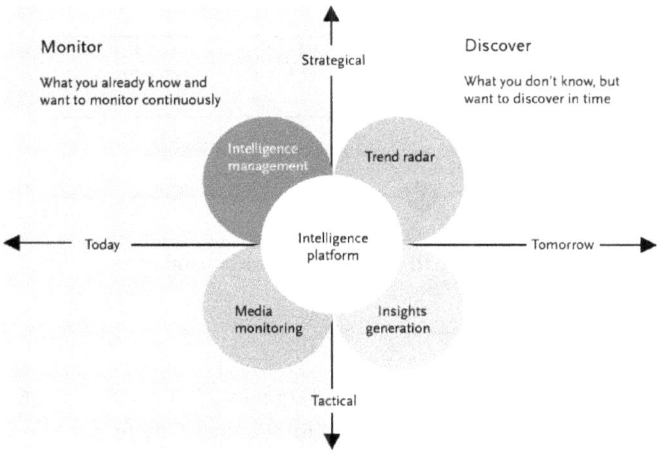

MCI platforms help you both to monitor and discover.

How do technology platforms support MCI?

You must construct the MCI platform to adhere to the organization's specific intelligence needs and working process of the MCI team. Today, it is common to find that organizations are reasonably good at collecting information but not as strong when structuring, analyzing, and collaborating about it. Survey data from 2019 SCIP participants illustrates this:

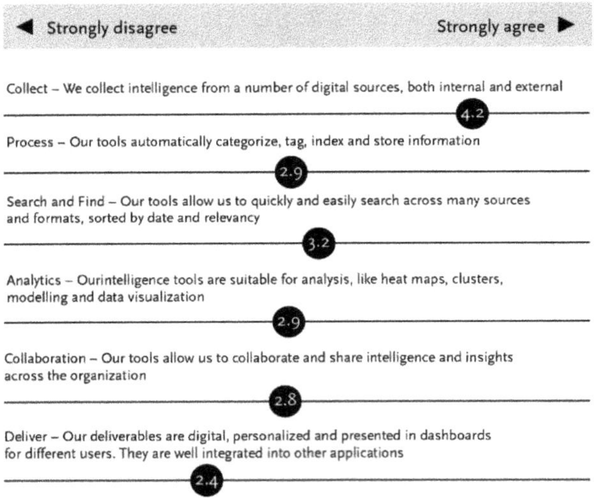
Strongly disagree
Strongly agree
Collect – We collect intelligence from a number of digital sources, both internal and external
4.2
Process – Our tools automatically categorize, tag, index and store information
2.9
Search and Find – Our tools allow us to quickly and easily search across many sources and formats, sorted by date and relevancy
3.2
Analytics – Ourintelligence tools are suitable for analysis, like heat maps, clusters, modelling and data visualization
2.9
Collaboration – Our tools allow us to collaborate and share intelligence and insights across the organization
2.8
Deliver – Our deliverables are digital, personalized and presented in dashboards for different users. They are well integrated into other applications
2.4

CI maturity level of organizations.[8]

---

[8] Source: SCIP conference, May 2019, Workshop "From the Age of Collectors to the Age of Augmented Intelligence," by Jesper Martell and Paul Santilli.

In today's world, intelligence users are many. Therefore, needs vary a lot between people, departments, and organizations. Some users just want to gain awareness or stay updated on a topic, while others seek very specific input to make career-defining decisions. Some users want to set up a monitoring exercise around a subject. Others want to get to the root of why business drivers change in a specific market. Intelligence functions look different in different organizations. Identified needs, resource availability, and organizational maturity impact how intelligence work is carried out and applied. To cope with varied needs and changes over time, a MCI platform must be flexible and easily adapt:

To cope with varied needs and changes over time, a MCI platform must be flexible and easily adapt.

MCI happens everywhere and at all times within an organization. The truth is this has always been the case. Still, digitalization, let alone AI, supercharges that, and intelligence "production" must cope with this dramatic change, one that enables asynchronous intelligence work. Decisions must be made faster and faster. Digitalization and new technologies have sped up this development so that any tools used must support this type of non-sequential intelligence work.

Consequently, a capable MCI platform will support the MCI team across all parts of the new Intelligence Web (as introduced in Chapter 2.1). In the following section, we will relate MCI platforms from the perspective of each of these seven parts.

Vision, goals, and strategy

In MCI terms, vision, goals, and strategy are very much about formulating the right questions and defining the intelligence needs of the organization. As the business environment changes, so does the purpose of MCI. This is an ongoing activity whereby a MCI platform is of tremendous support given it can quickly adapt to change. What you monitored yesterday might be irrelevant today. What you discover today might summon a different need for insights tomorrow.

Remind yourself of the purpose of market and competitive intelligence activities within the organization. The most common purposes are:

- Support decisions in increasing profitability and growth
- Create more efficient business tactics and strategies
- Speed up the decision-making process

Planning, needs, gaps, and direction

A MCI platform cannot spring from nothing. Rather, it must be told what to monitor and seek out decision-maker interests. Developing and maintaining a MCI classification involves both MCI professionals and users of intelligence to ensure "the lens" focuses on the strategic target of the organization. Going forward after the first initiation, the beauty of the classification is that it will, itself, help define its own development with its sheer power to support the MCI team in finding gaps or blind spots in the intelligence analysis. In summary, a well-operating MCI classification is the technology part of planning.

Collection of sources

An MCI platform is a technology tool that should significantly increase efficiency and quality of the MCI work. However, its "reading capacity" is one particular field of work in which the platform supersedes human capability by leaps and bounds. A MCI solution aggregates multiple information sources at a speed and scale unattainable by humans. It can read tens or hundreds of thousands of information sources and filter, categorize, and disseminate them without even the touch of a human hand. Sources may include news, blogs, reviews, market research, financial and patent filings, job postings, product information and pricing, advertising, website content, win/loss analysis, e-mail, marketing collateral, and much more.

In addition to handling large volumes of information, a MCI platform makes it easier for your organization's "Observers" or "Sensors" to report what they see and hear. Make sure your platform has a simple mobile interface so your Observers or Sensors can easily share insights at their leisure. For the MCI team, this means that while ensuring relevant and qualitative sources are fed into the platform, work can focus on interpreting patterns of information, drawing conclusions, and suggesting decisions to make—in short, spending time on analysis.

Processing and curating information

This is easy simply because a platform makes this step in the MCI cycle a non-issue. With a modern MCI platform in place, processing and storing information is automated. We classify by applying taxonomies and Machine Learning to add tags and topics. Search engines index and add context, making data searchable. In short, the MCI platform should do this job automatically for you.

Analysis and insights

Can technology tools really perform analysis? Can any IT system perform analysis? No, IT systems do not analyze!

They structure, calculate, read, and visualize a magnitude of more data than can be done by humans. Systems support human analysts in putting details into context. They help provide perspectives and are simply invaluable for making sense of bizarre amounts of information, but they do not analyze—people do!

IT systems do not analyze! They structure, calculate, read, and visualize a magnitude of more data than can be done by humans. Systems support human analysts in putting details into context. They help provide perspectives and are simply invaluable for making sense of bizarre amounts of information, but they do not analyze—people do!

Consequently, what one should truly expect from a MCI platform is a range of *analysis support tools*, such as:

- Visualizing
- Flagging
- Analyzing templates
- Benchmarking profiles

Sharing with all decision-makers

MCI platforms should enable users to streamline the production of deliverables and reports relevant to specific stakeholders: competitor intelligence, customer intelligence, or strategic intelligence. Alerts are a popular method for disseminating intelligence, but MCI solutions should have the capacity to go beyond the weekly newsletter to reach a wider audience within the organization. They contain templates, such as battlecards and competitor profiles, and can export visualizations such as word clouds, heat maps, or charts. Define a well-structured model for access rights to varied content. This serves three key purposes:

1. Manage copyright matters with your commercial content providers
2. Manage confidentiality matters for your internal content
3. Support your users in filtering content based on their needs

Actions and decisions

As a MCI team, the question to ask is, "Who are our MCI 'customers?'" A MCI professional is always there to support someone else's decision-making for the better, so the question really boils down to how to best support individual recipients of intelligence. Many MCI platform solutions support insight-to-action via integration with various third-party systems (e.g., CRM, web content management, and messaging) to deliver insights to decision-makers within applications they are already using.

After an insight is created and delivered, it is important to get feedback. Platforms should have usage statistics that track what is read (and by whom) to help analysts understand what decision-makers need.

Be part of an enterprise eco-system

We have emphasized that even if you execute brilliant analysis and produce clever insights, this has little value unless it reaches the right audience and decision-makers. Intelligence is only successful if it leads to action and change. This means it should be part of every employee's responsibilities, and everyone should share and have access to relevant intelligence about the business environment.

To accomplish this, establish multiple methods of providing intelligence to ensure insights are used and acted upon. It is much easier to reach decision-makers and share insights within applications they already use. But what is the best way to accomplish this? Time is very limited for most decision-makers, meaning you must reach them via channels and applications they already use. It is harder to get a busy executive to learn a new system or tool than to communicate with them using familiar ones like e-mail or mobile phones. What this means for MCI platforms is that they don't work well as standalone systems. They must be well embedded and integrated into the organization's eco-system of tools to make access easy using a preferred platform. We perform and apply MCI to many areas and functions within an organization, such as marketing, sales, customer insights, market research, product development, corporate strategy, and innovation. Depending on where MCI is consumed, the platform should smoothly integrate with multiple enterprise applications. These include, but are not limited to:

- **Collaboration platforms** (such as Slack, Teams, and e-mail). These types of collaboration and messaging platforms are becoming more and more popular ways to communicate and share information, insights, and observations within enterprises. All employees use them, and therefore, they are a natural channel for MCI to collect and distribute intelligence.

- **Content management systems** (such as SharePoint, Optimizely , or OpenText). These are perhaps the most common platforms used by organizations to spread information to employees via, for example, intranets and portals. They are therefore important to consider when implementing a MCI platform and deciphering content location.

- **Customer Relationship Management (CRM) tools** (such as Salesforce, Microsoft Dynamics, and Oracle). Competitive intelligence can help sales teams improve sales, sales decision-making, and win ratios by providing competitor profiles and battlecards. Sales will see the relevance of this for their CRM systems.

- **Business Intelligence (BI) tools** (such as Tableaux and Microsoft Power BI). Analysts typically use these to visualize large volumes of structured and numerical information. BI tools complement MCI platforms very well, and therefore, both benefit from integration.

- **Enterprise Resource Planning (ERP) systems** (such as SAP and Oracle). These enterprise IT systems manage internal data about company operations. Note that viewing data from internal ERP and BI systems often means looking at the past. A MCI platform will give your organization a tool that focuses on understanding future scenarios.

- **Knowledge Management systems**. If there is an ongoing Knowledge Management (KM) initiative within your organization, we recommend linking up with it. If not, the recommendation is to liaise with IT, propose a KM initiative, and employ the intelligence operation as its first user application. There is lots to gain by seeing MCI and KM as complementary activities and absolutely nothing wrong with MCI as the driving force behind corporate KM initiatives.

Viewing data from internal ERP and BI systems means looking at the past.

In technical terms, consider these two main areas to enable integration when building an MCI platform:

- **Single Sign-On (SSO)** is a user authentication process that permits a user to enter one name and password to access multiple applications/resources. With the help of SSO, a user can move seamlessly between applications they use most often.

- An **Application Programming Interface (API)** is a concept to integrate computer systems on a programming level. APIs provide the tools to publish or extract data between different platforms. "APIs create business agility that fosters the rapid business reconfiguration necessary to continually adapt to an unknown future, revamp customer experience, address regulatory challenges, respond to new and changing competition, and react to a wide range of unpredictable scenarios."[9]

[9] Forrester Research, The Forrester Wave™: API Management Solutions, Q4 2018.

Checklist for evaluating a MCI platform

Based on our experience with hundreds of MCI platforms, we have compiled a checklist of requirements and considerations when selecting a suitable MCI platform for your organization. This list of 14 areas is not exhaustive nor detailed but rather intended to serve as inspiration.

We won't detail the strengths and weaknesses of MCI platform providers, but the bottom line is that no provider is everything to everybody. MCI technology vendor approaches vary concerning features and functions, technology, and go-to-market strategy depending on your maturity level.

- Some include content and some connect to content
- Many focus on external information from the web while others gather internal knowledge or use both external and internal sources
- Some focus on creating reports, tactical battlecards, and newsletters, while others concern themselves with future-oriented analytics

Which platform works best for your organization depends on its purpose and maturity. We find the best MCI platforms are ones specifically designed to support the entire competitive intelligence process.

The best MCI platforms are ones specifically designed to support the entire competitive intelligence process.

1. User Experience
Intuitive, functional, and user-friendly visual interface, with customizable dashboards for different user groups
Can it be company branded?
Is there personalization? An ability to create personalized e-mail alerts?
Can admins implement design changes (layout, categories, and newsletters)?
How is mobility supported (access via smartphones and tablets)?
Can different user roles exist?
2. Content Management
Content management platform with a broad functionality of automatic and manual document categorization into competitors, customers, information type, countries, etc.
A workflow for curating content using favorite lists and collaborative reports
Approval process for article publishing (users can upload documents and administrators decide which articles should be published)
How can information from the field be collected?
3. Content Aggregation/Classification
Automatic content aggregation: automatic retrieval of information and news from a wide range of external sources
Ability to connect content from internal and external sources
Is information manually and/or automatically categorized and converted into one common format without manual upload and copy and paste?

How does the platform approach data/information categorization/tagging? What is manual, predefined, and automatic?
4. Search
Full text search (including attachments) with Boolean logic
Is there date and relevancy sorting?
How do the tool's AI-enabled search features and functions curate, classify, recommend, and distribute content? Does this differ by user role or use case?
Possibility to saved searches
How are different languages addressed?
How are duplicates addressed?
Ability to rank results by date/relevancy
5. Collaboration
Interactive dialog platform (add comments and recommend articles)
Which collaboration features and functions are available within the tool today? Is there an ability to like, rate, vote, or share content?
Is there a way to find people and subject matter experts?
Ability to create dashboards for different groups of users?
6. Sources
Which sources are available out of the box?
How can you add your own sources?
How are social media channels integrated?
7. Alerts and Newsletters
Customized newsletter function (design/recipients and group/different layouts to choose)
Possibility to create personal alerts
Possibility for admin to set up suggested alerts
8. Access Rights and Security
Access rights at different levels (readers, publishers, admin, etc.) including access groups
Are penetration tests available, and the results shown?

Is the platform GDPR-compliant? How is personal data addressed?
How is system security ensured?
Is data encryption available?
Ability to approve articles before publication
9. Usage Statistics
Usage statistics, topic statistics generated automatically, e.g., number of users, logins, articles read, alerts
Ability to administrate users
10. Data hosting
What are the data storage capabilities?
Is Single Sign On possible?
Where are the servers hosted (countries and provider, ISO certification available)?
11. Data Migration and Integrations
Automatic data migration from existing platforms
What are the capabilities for third-party integrations, e.g., APIs for CRM, BI?
Can content be exported to PDF, RSS, MS Office?
12. Analytics and Artificial Intelligence
Automatic data visualization (charts, diagrams if data available) (company financials, market sizing, etc.)
Ability to benchmark templates
Visualizing data through charts and heat maps
Word clouds
Sentiment analysis
How do AI-based summaries, classification, and recommendations work?
13. Services and Support
How is Change/Incident Management organized (ticket system; employees; 1st, 2nd, and 3rd-level support)?
Which Service Level Agreements are supported?
What kind of training is available?

How is Change/Incident Management organized (ticket system; employees; 1st, 2nd, and 3rd-level support)?
14. Product Vision and Future Road Map
Does the provider have a long-term vision for its product?
How important is the product versus other products and services offered by the provider?
Can the solution scale and grow with your needs?
What reference customers are available?

Table: 14-point checklist for evaluating MCI platforms.

Main challenges in deploying MCI technology

There are challenges in making technology work and delivering benefits, as you can see in this word cloud based on an interactive 2019 SCIP survey.

The main challenges in deploying MCI tools.[10]

10 Source: Ejdling-Martell SCIP workshop, 2019.

Three of the biggest challenges you must consider and overcome are:

Challenge No. 1: You need to do some thinking

The MCI platform may be advertised as an off-the-shelf solution, but remember that the tool's main function is to collect, process, and disseminate information. The intelligence you deliver will still require some level of analysis.

The right MCI platform should provide valuable information with little to no setup. It may be somewhat generic and lack customizable options, but it will provide value. However, receiving out-of-the-box insights from a new software tool is simply not realistic. You must remember the process will require time and iteration. Consider the long-term gains and understand the payoff will come—making sure management understands the same.

Challenge No. 2: You need new ways of working

Beginnings are full of optimism. Everyone is on their best behavior in a new relationship. The excitement of "something new" can be blinding… and then, suddenly, the honeymoon is over and optimized work is required. It may feel unfamiliar, uncomfortable, and less efficient. You're tempted to go back to the way things were when you knew what to expect.

Challenge No. 3: You need to integrate

You believe you can personally customize the software. You confidently begin the onboarding process, but as you work through it, face the dawning realization that you're in over your head and need help. Now you must hire a software company or freelancer to implement sought-after customizations, and neither of these expenses is part of your budget.

No, the sales rep didn't mislead you, nor did you misunderstand the information you were presented. The fact is, many things, on the surface, seem less complicated than they actually are. So, if a specific customization is important for your ability to gather the market research you need, make sure you clearly understand this before purchasing the required tools and assigning roles accordingly.

The biggest, and probably most costly, mistake you can make is to lock yourself into a system that cannot grow with your organization as it develops.

Key takeaways

Summarizing the key takeaways of this chapter:

- The key purpose of a MCI platform is to provide a single access point to both external and internal sources for all producers and consumers of intelligence within your organization.

- A MCI platform should be much more than simply monitoring web news and producing newsletters detailing past events. In addition to monitoring, MCI platforms should have the capability to support MCI in the discovery and creation of new insights.

- To cope with varied needs and changes over time, an MCI platform must be flexible and easily adapt to new requirements.

- MCI platforms don't work well as stand-alone systems. They must be well embedded and integrated into the organization's eco-system of tools to ensure easy access from the user's preferred platform.

- Find inspiration in the checklist of 14 points to consider when evaluating MCI platforms.

CHAPTER 8

How to Apply Artificial Intelligence and Machine Learning Technology[11]

We develop a structure, define sources, and deploy a software platform to cater to structures and information. What may be lost in the above yet on everyone's radar these days? Artificial Intelligence or AI for short.

For many, AI is the answer to every conceivable question. Yet, approaching the topic less populistically uncovers a tremendously capable technology but one that dictates in-depth knowledge and significant planning and configuration to be of any use at all. Even AI applications must understand the questions to answer to produce

[11] Parts of this chapter are taken from "Machine Learning Implications for Intelligence and Insights: Man versus Machine: How can new technologies augment our intelligence capabilities? " by Jesper Martell and Paul Santilli, SCIP Magazine, Fall 2017, Nov 29, 2017.

valuable output, and AI algorithms have not yet succeeded in first posing the questions.

A large part of AI lies in so-called Machine Learning (ML). Put in the perspective of Chapter 5's discussion on structure and classifications, Machine Learning is a technology that supports classification via algorithms. This chapter describes Machine Learning, its role in the context of MCI, and how it can be applied to solve intelligence problems.

Machine Learning is often expressed in different ways (e.g., Artificial Intelligence (AI), predictive analytics, data-mining, deep learning, forecasting, Natural Language Processing, and simulations), but basically, it's about algorithms that analyze data to find models used to predict outcomes or understand the context with pin-point accuracy, improving or "learning" as more information becomes available. The question is how we can apply this in the intelligence world.

The new digitized world

Machine Learning and Artificial Intelligence are not new concepts, so why are they now so important for intelligence professionals and analysts? The simple reason is that we live in a sociological era unlike any other in history. Through the use of technology, not only are new products developed that change the way we use tools, but it has changed sociological and behavior patterns in humans. Our communication, interaction, social engagement, and networks are all revolutionized through digitized society development. Within roughly 10-15 years, since the middle of the first decade of the 21st century, a complete paradigm shift has occurred in how people communicate. A complete behavior change has ensued within a very short window of time, with an extraordinary rate of adoption for new technology that immediately pervades the social lexicon of mankind—and the rate of change is accelerating. This dramatically impacts the challenge for organizations to adopt and understand the technology and apply it to compete within this environment effectively.

Interestingly, unlike in historical times when more developed and technologically savvy countries and geographical regions of the world were able to harness new technologies quicker than other "less evolved" areas, digitized technology adoption is now literally borderless. This results in the globalization of a digitized society at an unprecedented scale. New ideas and applications travel at the speed of the internet. Multi-billion dollar "game changing" companies rise and fall based on the newest technological disruption that is now almost a monthly "expectation," rather than a revolutionary generational development.

The barriers to entry are extremely low—no longer do incubation companies rely on an influx of huge venture capital resources and funding to grow their ideas and gain traction in markets dominated by corporate giants. Rather, those digitized ventures undermine steadfast corporate fixtures by 1) understanding this digitized environment and 2) out maneuvering these giants by overlapping a digitized capability atop a brick-and-mortar foundation.

Transforming ideas into value is how today's environment defines success. The ability to learn quickly and anticipate the future of the market are critical success factors. However, one underlying element is universal and absolute: time—the differentiator no matter which industry you occupy. It isn't just about the ability of these companies to execute a good idea, but the *inability* of established fixtures within the industry to act quickly and transform their own business models to compete. This is due to either 1) not seeing the push towards digitization, 2) seeing but ignoring the push and not wanting to leave their "comfort zone," or 3) seeing and responding but not fully understanding implications and requirements and missing the key factor we previously mentioned—the time required for execution. The ability to pivot during this disruption is what differentiates "nimble" organizations from those that are "static" and slow to respond. In today's world, every company is at risk of missing a market opportunity, not securing their enterprise, and facing disruption from a new idea or business model.

The ability to pivot during this disruption is what differentiates "nimble" organizations from those that are "static" and slow to respond. In today's world, every company is at risk of missing a market opportunity, not securing their enterprise, and facing disruption from a new idea or business model.

We now live in a comprehensive digitized society. With the upcoming maturity of the "Internet of Things" and connectivity associated with this concept, billions of people can potentially connect with billions of devices. The sheer scope of the data analytics challenge is readily apparent and overwhelming! "Time to Insight" and "Time to Execution" are more critical than ever, as the ability to respond to market disruptions quickly evolves from months and years to days and weeks.

Disrupting the intelligence world

Through the eyes of an intelligence professional, the business climate presents increasing challenges. The onslaught of never-ending data, proliferation of incubation test beds, and rise of internet business disruptors seemingly overnight dramatically impacts the intelligence professional's ability to not only acquire the right data but synthesize analytics to draw accurate conclusions—all while navigating an uninterrupted, fluid information environment. Sequential analytics processing is a thing of the past. The business climate moves so fast that organizations must incorporate intelligence and analytics as an integral part of their organizations, wherein ongoing data collection, synthesis, and integration with company strategy is a routine activity.

Unfortunately, intelligence communities are often trapped within the customary mold of common methodologies, fragmented infrastructure hierarchy, and limited ability to influence company direction. To truly apply intelligence at a universal level, corporations must take a pragmatic stance to leverage intelligence and analysis efforts throughout the organization, recognizing the value of systemic approaches to intertwine intelligence with overall company strategy.

The fundamental key differentiator is generating executable insights faster than competitors and acting upon those insights at the right moment. History is fraught with examples of premature or mistimed product/technology introductions plagued by miscues due to poor intelligence, delayed decision-making, and ill-conceived execution tactics and strategies. However, it's also rich in introductions that have successfully mastered this challenge—first and foremost, by understanding the technology curve, gathering insights, and embracing business disruption challenges while identifying new growth opportunities. This places many CEOs in an extremely uncomfortable position—the need to think outside of their business core competencies and take strategic action that may exist far outside revenue-generating functions. Of course, risks and uncertainty often outweigh the decision to move tangentially, but organizations cannot take the huge risk of "disruption impact avoidance" with heads buried in the sand, praying it does not affect their company—especially in today's digitized society!

The fundamental key differentiator is the ability to generate executable insights faster than competitors.

There are three key questions:

- What is the potential for this new idea?
- What information do I need to add to our business strategy?
- How fast can I monetize the opportunity?

So, how does an intelligence organization capitalize on this information-rich digitized society to provide content so organizations can act? The challenge is the ability to acquire, process, and analyze data on a seemingly real-time basis. Realistic? Not entirely, but mechanisms are present to help shift modeling behavior further down the timescale axis and into an environment where analytics is performed more frequently: and with better accuracy than traditional "batch" processing algorithms often used by the intelligence community.

A new and exciting capability exists, automating the collection of pertinent information and subsequent downstream "learnings" of the data pool. Utilizing tools to gather and process this data through large central data repositories (Knowledge Management Systems, Business Information Systems, Customer Databases, etc.) is now a necessity. However, coupled with this is the ability to apply Machine Learning to subsequently "predict" business behavior and automate much of the process, resulting in nimbler organizations and providing actionable insights more quickly. This is where organizations see the biggest return on investment when faced with the daunting challenges of a digitized society.

Introducing AI and ML

We all know and feel that the volume of available information has and will continue to grow exponentially. However, simultaneously, the computational power and storage capabilities of machines are gaining steam quickly, with more sophisticated algorithms available to sift through all this data.

We have arrived at a point where we begin to ask ourselves if machines can actually think for us. While the concept of Artificial Intelligence has been around for a long time (see image below), recent advances in algorithms, processing power, and exponential growth in available information give rise to machines with unprecedented capabilities.

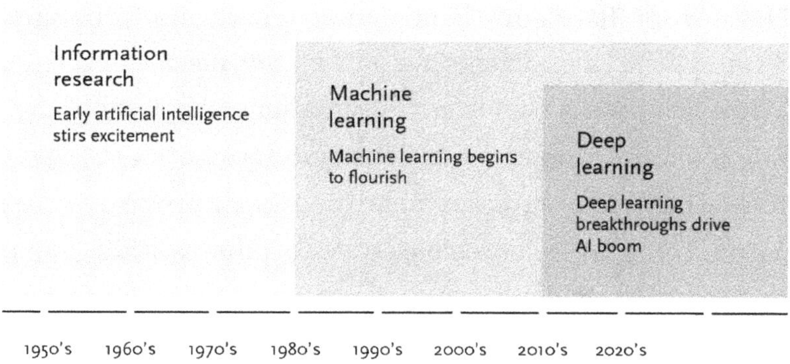

Machine Learning is seen as a subset of Artificial Intelligence.

While these technologies might not actually "think" in the traditional sense, machines are beginning to perform tasks typically considered the sole domain of humans—and sometimes at a superior level. Suddenly, meaningful AI does not seem so far away. It represents a broad computer science field that simulates aspects of human intelligence, while Machine Learning refers to the process of using algorithms to accomplish a specific task.

Let's focus on how Machine Learning can be applied to solve intelligence problems. Machine Learning is often expressed in different ways (e.g., Artificial Intelligence, predictive analytics, data-mining, deep learning, forecasting, Natural Language Processing and simulations), but is centered around algorithms that analyze data to find models that can predict outcomes or understand context with significant accuracy, improving or "learning" as more information becomes available.

Developers hard-code conventional software programs with specific instructions for tasks they need to execute. While this works well in many situations, this type of top-down instruction has limitations and does not evolve over time. The human programmer cannot code provisions that account for every possible state of the world. If the environment changes, software programs will malfunction or cease to be relevant. In contrast, it is possible to create algorithms that "learn" from data and, if necessary, evolve and adapt to new circumstances without the need for explicit reprogramming. The concept underpinning Machine Learning is to feed the algorithm with "experiences" (training data) and a generalized learning strategy, allowing it to glean patterns, associations, and insights from the data—in short, *training* the system rather than *programming* it.

Remember, AI is not magic; it's logic.

So, what is an algorithm?

Because algorithms are at the core of Machine Learning, it is important to understand how they work as an area for intelligence professionals to apply their expertise. Machine Learning-generated algorithms (models) are functions that take input variables and apply formulas or rules to predict an outcome.

Algorithm

$$Y = f(X)$$

Y = Predicted outcome (validation, approval)

f = Prediction function (model)

X = Input variables (data)

An algorithm is a sequence of instructions telling a computer what to do.

Thus, in technical terms, an algorithm is a sequence of instructions that tell a computer what to do. Here is a concrete example of an algorithm that a computer can use for playing tic-tac-toe, with the likeable property that it never loses!

- If your opponent has 2 in a row, play on the remaining square.

- Otherwise, if there is a move that creates 2 lines of 2 in a row, play that.
- Otherwise, if the center square is free, play there.
- Otherwise, if your opponent has played in a corner, play in the opposite corner.
- Otherwise, if there is an empty corner, play there.
- Otherwise, play on an empty square.

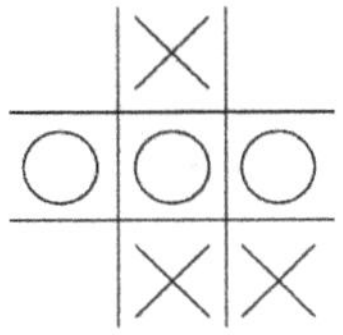

Example of an algorithm that never loses.

Algorithms can be very powerful and intelligent but have the following limitations:

- They are based on probabilities (such as 66% chance that you will like a particular TV show)

- They cannot accurately predict all questions (such as elections, macroeconomics, and disasters)

- They are based on data from the past and are not necessarily causative

- They rely heavily on a supply of relevant data that is preferably stable and consistent

- They will produce low-quality results if supplied with low-quality data

Applying machine learning to intelligence challenges

All Machine Learning algorithms require large amounts of training data ("experiences") to learn. They recognize training data patterns and develop a "model" of the world the data describes. Reinforcement learning is slightly different from other techniques. Training data is not fed to the algorithm but generated in real-time via interactions with and feedback from the environment. But in all cases, as new training data comes in, the algorithm can improve and refine the model. This is particularly well suited to solve three types of intelligence challenges: classification, recommendation/prediction, and clustering.

1.Classification	Identifies information as x, y, or z, classifying and/or labeling it.
2.Recommendation/Prediction	Recommends the best action or content. Predicts the probability of future action based on historical data.
3.Clustering	Finds patterns or similarities in information and segments into clusters. Discovers associations (e.g., people who read certain books).

Three types of Intelligence challenges solved by Machine Learning.

First, tackling classification problems involves making observations, such as identifying objects in images and video or recognizing text and audio. From an intelligence perspective, this can help tremendously when reading and analyzing large volumes of text to determine the "who," "what," "when" and "where." When searching for information, ML can, for example, identify "trending themes" or the most widely "talked about" subjects in a body of text. Human analysts can then use this intelligence to determine the "why" and set an appropriate course of action.

Second, Machine Learning can also be employed for recommendations and predictions, such as estimating the likelihood of events and forecasting outcomes. This could, for example, be very helpful for an analyst looking to predict the chance of a competitor launching a new product at a specific point in time.

Third, Machine Learning can be used to segment data into clusters according to association. An intelligence application can detect and extract sentiment on a more accurate level automatically, such as whether this news is positive or negative, or whether this event is a strength or weakness for us. Applied to a MCI environment, this can have extremely favorable outcomes. ML can automate many areas of data synthesis and significantly help arrive at quicker "Times to Insight" over traditional methods:

- Automation classification analytics involving vast quantities of data, performed in real-time within online tools and databases
- Templates/analytics algorithm foundations used as a basis for ML data population (automating this process fosters "real-time" processing)
- Clustering techniques for data pattern recognition promote quicker content and deliverable development

---

Machine Learning can automate many areas of data synthesis and significantly help arrive at quicker "Times to Insight" over traditional methods.

Tool structure is key here—utilizing a robust IT-based internet-interactive ML capability will automate, provide better content and yield better quality, faster results. Additionally, learning algorithms can be built into the tool design to continually improve and become automated/more efficient.

Use cases of machine learning

You probably don't even realize it, but Machine Learning already surrounds us. Whenever you use a computer device, the chances are high that ML is involved. ML prevents your e-mail from overloading with spam and helps you buy Amazon books and select Netflix films, avoid rush hour traffic, find and translate Google information, check spelling and grammar in Microsoft Word, find Facebook friends, win chess games and much, much more.

Digital giants such as Google, Facebook, Netflix, and Baidu, and industrial companies such as Intel and GE are leading the way in these innovations, seeing Machine Learning as fundamental to their core business and strategy. The most immediate area for businesses is how to apply Machine Learning algorithms and where they will likely have the biggest impact. Which kinds of intelligence problems is Machine Learning best suited to tackle?

Its potential applications are remarkably broad. The value capacity is everywhere, even extending into sectors typically slow to apply data and analytics. As this technology is further adopted, it can generate tremendous productivity gains and improved quality of life. However, it could also unleash a wave of job losses and other disruptions, not to mention thorny ethical and societal questions to address as machines gain greater intellectual capabilities.

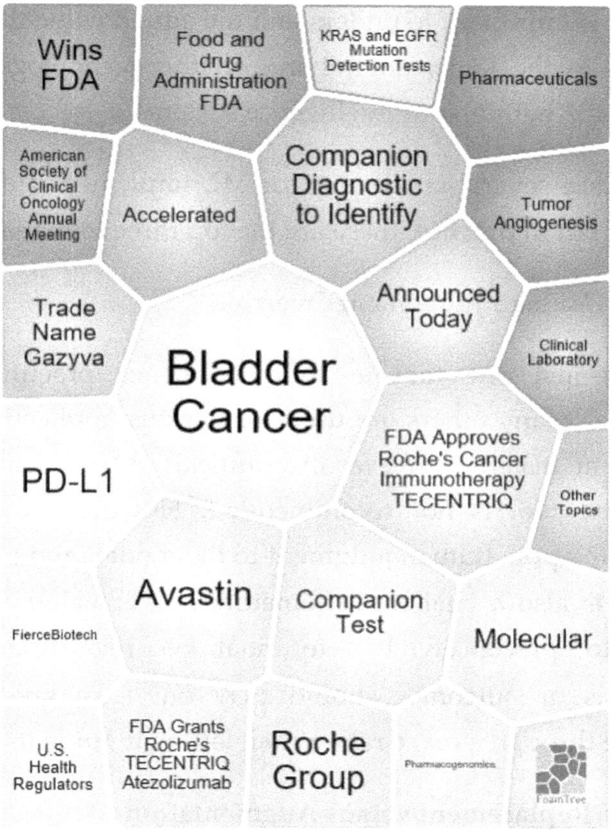

Thanks to Machine Learning, a search for Roche, Oncology and FDA provides a cluster of results wherein the main trends are immediately visible and easier to analyze.

Machine learning risks

There are areas where, if not appropriately applied and managed, Machine Learning can present problems. This is why it is important to understand the added value that ML brings to the table, not relying on this technology as a "cure-all" within your intelligence systems.

There are several challenges for ML implementation and usage, but in practice, these are the top three to manage:

1) **Human Judgement Override**

ML is just one tool in the intelligence practitioner's toolbox. Many others are used for various applications to arrive at insight and execution quickly. Overreliance on any one tool is not recommended. However, knowing when to apply human judgment to the model (and at what level) is also a challenge. Sometimes, overzealous use is due to preconceived determinations regarding how analysis or outcomes should play out (like guiding a mouse through a maze rather than letting it guide itself).

2) **Replacement versus Augmentation**

In theory, all ML learning should ultimately result in a "single" point of knowledge. That is, regardless of any situation you arrive at the same outcome dictated by the algorithms. But, of course, this is highly impractical in a real-world scenario. Therefore, ML must work in combination with other algorithms and tools, including human intelligence. The objective here is to augment your toolbox with valuable ML capabilities to help you anticipate industry and competitive behaviors within overall intelligence modeling.

3) **Specialized Learning versus Generalized Learning**

There are applications for both, but understanding where to use them is the key to success. Some ML capabilities are confined to specific components of the intelligence model, while others can holistically provide industry and global knowledge. Sometimes, users may over apply ML to less suitable areas for ML algorithm design, thus polluting findings from other tools and compromising results. Understanding how to apply specific ML functions that integrate with your overall analysis is the desired objective for intelligence professionals.

Will machines replace humans?

Will Machine Learning and Artificial Intelligence replace us in the future? This is a million-dollar question that is subject to frequent debate.

In fact, we do not believe ML/AI will replace intelligence analysts anytime soon. Artificial intelligence is currently in the initial stages of prototyping, fixing, and testing all errors. Further, events exist that ML/AI simply cannot predict, as described in the book *The Black Swan*. If you only ever feed a computer white swans, it will inherently calculate zero probability of seeing a black one.

Events exist that ML/AI simply cannot predict. If you only ever feed a computer white swans, it will inherently calculate zero probability of seeing a black one.

On the positive side, intelligence professionals should actively use and test available ML to experience it and foster better applications as technology evolves. ML can already help analysts skip the "boring" work, enhancing their focus and knowledge. If you possess smart analysts and resources to use intelligent tools, you will see the best results. However, ML may replace specific roles in the future. The first people upended will likely be those who lack creativity and fulfill task-based roles.

McKinsey Global Institute[12] has defined a new work role that would suit intelligence professionals very well: the so-called **Business Translator.** "Business Translators serve to link analytical talent and practical applications to business questions. In addition to boasting data-savvy qualities, Business Translators must possess deep organizational knowledge and industry or functional expertise. This

---

[12] Source: McKinsey Global Institute, "The Age of Analytics: Competing in a Data-Driven World," DECEMBER 2016.

enables them to ask the data science team the right questions and derive the right insights from their findings. It may be possible to outsource analytics activities, but Business Translator roles require proprietary knowledge and should be more deeply embedded into the organization." McKinsey estimates a need for 2-4 million Business Translators in the US alone over the next decade.

Humans vs Machines		
	Humans	Machines
Collect	★	★ ★ ★ ★
Process	★ ★ ★ ★	★ ★ ★
Analyze	★ ★	★
Deliver	★ ★	★ ★ ★

Humans and machines have different feature sets

Use them in stepwise iterations

Humans + Machines=
Augmented intelligence

Augmented Intelligence				
Collect	★	★	★	★	★
Process	★	★	★	★	★
Analyze	★	★	★	★	★
Deliver	★	★	★	★	★

From Data to Insights

Augmented intelligence will allow you to discover insights and early warning signals

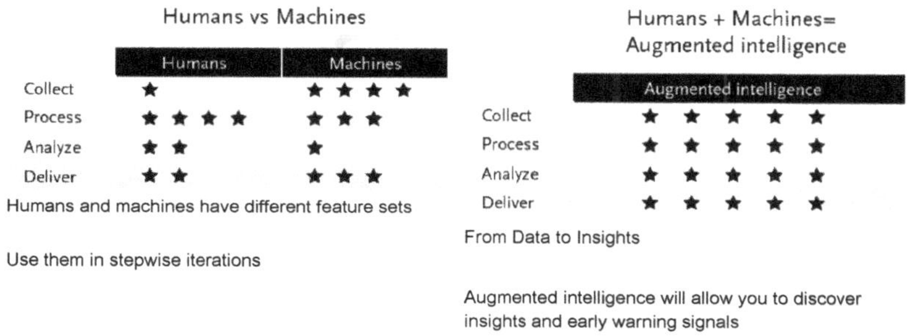

Augmented Intelligence - Humans and Machines have different strengths that augment each other. Together they become unbeatable.

Towards augmented intelligence

Augmented Intelligence for Market and Competitive Intelligence uses computational algorithms to help the human end-user occupy the best position to make informed decisions.

Global economic and social systems have greatly changed in the last ten years, with the digital world growing at an exponential rate. There is the potential for 7+ billion people to connect through billions of machines, resulting in unprecedented quantities of data. Any analytical effort aims to leverage information and ask the right questions to improve business results. Now more than ever, decision-makers require improved ways to do this and extract actionable intelligence from ever-evolving information.

This is where Machine Learning-based intelligence systems can support users by empowering them to identify information, trends, and patterns that warrant attention. This new technology is more than an interesting phenomenon—it is indeed a requirement. But ML will not replace intelligence professionals who ask the right questions and put information in context. Rather than replacing humans, ML will augment human intelligence and enable people to become experts and cull insights much faster than before.

- Augmented Intelligence are **machine-**based algorithms that aid the **human** end-user in making informed decisions.

- Algorithms can read and analyze huge volumes of data and determine the "**who,**" "**what,**" "**when,**" and "**where.**"

- Humans use intelligence to interpret and determine the "**why,**" deciding on appropriate actions.

- To extract "**Actionable Intelligence**" from ever-evolving data types, decision-makers need robust ways to address decision-making and knowledge-gathering tasks.

Challenges with augmented intelligence applications

Augmented Intelligence for Market and Competitive Intelligence uses computational algorithms to help put the human end-user in the best position to make informed decisions. The purpose of a content recommender is to provide an Augmented Intelligence tool that overcomes the challenge of filtering an overwhelming amount of unstructured content.

Machine Learning-based recommenders are not a new concept. In fact, many implementations are currently used for commercial purposes, such as Amazon. These available models are optimized to structure data sets and classify product categories of data items to help shoppers find information and products they might enjoy, with the goal of selling more. However, when applying these models to short-lived unstructured data sets, they fall short.

Shopping-based applications can recommend products based on user purchase and data ratings to compute the similarity between users and items. The typical approach is often the nearest neighboring product(s) based on recommendations in a trust-based network of people: users employ their social network to acquire information and trusted relationships to filter it. On an e-commerce site, these people are strangers but form a temporary network in a customer group, in relation to the vendor and products sold.

Unlike shopping websites that boast established products and many classification terms, a content recommender for Market and Competitive Intelligence purposes must work within much shorter time spans and handle vast quantities of new content. The recommender might utilize tagged and content-rich documents, such as internal and external analysis reports with a months-long lifespan, but find it trickier to work with short-lived news items only available for a few hours or days. Additionally, consumer patterns vary from seeking or buying products in an online store.

An online retailer can collect usage patterns for a specific product over a long time from many users. A news and intelligence content recommender must work within quick timeframes and address fewer users and interactions.

There are many possible data points to explore when it comes to intelligence sources:

- Of course, the number of clicks can indicate a point of interest to a user but does not necessarily indicate the quality of the information.

- A rating system, such as thumbs-up, likes, or stars, might also boost the quality and relevancy rank, but corporate systems usually find it challenging to encourage people to upvote and recommend information on a scale that would be really helpful in its own right.

- The amount of time spent visiting an article is perhaps another important indicator, but these numbers might vary depending on the length of the content.

- Collaborative filtering based on clicks, deep readings, ratings, sharing, and other actions such as printing, exporting content, or user hash-tagging content is important.

The more metadata available, the better—some premium content providers already assign additional quantities of this to their articles. However, the bulk of content does not provide metadata, and Machine Learning technologies should analyze content to enrich it at the time of processing.

Organizations should apply a hybrid collaborative filtering model and several Machine Learning technologies to provide knowledge workers with up-to-date recommendations. The applied models must consider user metadata, content metadata, and interactions between them.

Key takeaways

Summarizing the key takeaways of this chapter:

- Augmented Intelligence for Market and Competitive Intelligence uses computational algorithms to help place the human end-user in the best position to make informed decisions.

- AI/ML supports but does not replace human analysis.

- Ask AI the right question, and you will be greatly rewarded. Ask AI the wrong question, and the opposite holds true.

CHAPTER 9

How to Create an Intelligent Community of People

With all tools, techniques, information, processes, and methodologies now implemented, what remains is the final step to really maximize the business value of resources and capabilities developed under the MCI umbrella. Communities lacking most of the above are almost doomed to fail as the fundamental driving force behind an Intelligent Community is making participants' work easier, more interesting, and adding more value to the organization all at once. For this to happen, the "plumbing" must be in place.

Intelligent Communities zero in on management, while underlying support systems are merely enabling tools. This chapter addresses managerial aspects of gathering individuals to become integral cogs in the MCI process/community machine.

Defining an intelligent community

The ultimate MCI target is to organizationally embed intelligence operations to "infiltrate" the organization's modus operandi so that they are almost no longer perceived as a distinct process. Rather, a core part of all company activity. Still, this component of the modus operandi must be managed, supported, and further nurtured. We opt to call this management model an Intelligent Community.

Building and managing an Intelligent Community is the art of balancing people's creativity with the structure of information. Both "Intelligent" and Community" are well-defined words in dictionaries. For example, the Concise Oxford Dictionary provides the following definitions (in summary):

Community

- A body of people with a common profession
- Fellowship of interests
- Joint ownership or liability

Intelligent

- Quick of mind, clever
- Able to vary behavior in response to unique situations, requirements, and past experience
- Having its own data-processing capability

The key bullets to consider are Community (3) and Intelligent (2and 3): thus, *a group of people, having joint ownership or liability, with its own processing capability and ability to vary behavior according to needs and experience.* In other words, this defines a group with a given task and a clear mandate to manage this in a way deemed suitable under each circumstance.

The definition of an Intelligent Community is "a network of trained knowledge workers who systematically work together to maximize the value of their combined knowledge." Intelligent Communities exist as organized network functions such as: global account management, purchasing, research, product development, human resources, business development, sales, and marketing—to name a few. In this book, the function of MCI operations prevails.

An Intelligent Community is a network of trained knowledge workers who systematically work together to maximize the value of their combined knowledge.

To build, manage and cultivate Intelligent Communities, two major issues must be addressed:

- balancing the creativity of people with the structure of information

- ensuring the community is an organized network for all members rather than an individual network that serves the purpose of only a few

In our garden, the entire eco system must benefit. Again, it is also worthwhile to stress the inevitability of enabling capabilities in all three ITP components simultaneously: **Information, Technology, and People**. An Intelligent Community depends on all three and will never be better than the chain's weakest link.

The intelligent community and its operations

From a management perspective, the first thing that must occur when considering Intelligent Community development is that the chief gardener (i.e., our Director of MCI) now also assumes the community manager role. Although a community is supposed to operate independently, it needs its modus operandi to be fully transparent and unanimous. That is the key responsibility of the community manager, ***not*** to assign community tasks. These can, and should, be triggered from any corner of the Community. This, of course, includes the Community manager, but not to a greater extent than any other participant. Recall the dictionary definitions, "Able to vary behavior in response to unique situations, requirements, and past experience" and "Having its own data-processing capability," as the notions of "intelligent." This should apply to an Intelligent Community as an entity, without requiring the "manager" to intervene in the task-decision process. Furthermore, each task very rarely will involve more than a few Community members at each time.

Thus, individuals who find themselves in business situations requiring community support should be able to:

- Immediately choose the right community (one can participate in multiple communities), and

- Within that Community, immediately identify and make contact with the team that can help solve this particular issue in the most efficient and competitive way

Now, this may sound straightforward enough, but it is truly when Community management comes into play. Not to help in each particular instance, that is, but to ensure each community participant can do this at all times and locations. This means ensuring the community structure is crystal clear and transparent at all times and participants are happy to help with such tasks (not just expecting support). Ultimately, there is a need to manage the community's agreed-upon modus operandi to ensure each team is not required to spend time addressing issues from time to time, but rather the ability to focus on the business issue at hand instantly.

Managing a community involves three specific organizational capabilities. These are always the same no matter the type of community, but the content of each one may in fact vary:

- Utilization of information resources
- Utilization of human resources
- Development and maintenance of methodologies

Managing intelligent communities—Information resources

In previous chapters, we elaborated extensively on information management, solely focusing on platform creation and information flow. However, a key part of Community management is ensuring this asset is also used properly. Half of the work in enabling this capability is structuring the information and communication platform per business requirements. The second piece is a continuous task for every community manager—training and internal marketing for this resource.

For Intelligent Communities to operate efficiently and provide value, the information and communication flow must have a structure that reflects each specific community mandate. Many required information-related capabilities were outlined earlier in this book. Still, there are two additional perspectives to consider when managing Intelligent Communities: broad usage throughout the organization and niche usage by community specialists.

Most ***broad usage*** will rarely extend beyond news services, trade newsletters, and business magazine content. Some decision-makers may, after some time, use more easily accessible market research reports and analysis findings that are made available. Still, this day-to-day newsfeed and research utilization is valuable in harnessing your community information flow according to the analytical structure and reaching a large group of people, raising general business awareness while connecting non-community members to your thinking. As one usually cannot train 1,000 people in information utility, it is rather a question of internal marketing. Leverage all channels such as company internal chats, team sites, magazines, CCTV, general internal websites, etc. Furthermore, the MCI specific site, or channel, must have some "attractions" to draw attention. These can vary: "This week's poll" on various issues, "games" or gamifications related to your business, general updated CEO statements, or any other "front page" attractions of general interest that align with your MCI service. One may almost see this as a media planning activity.

Niche usage should fall within your Intelligent Community. This is where training comes in! Invite authors from external sources for training sessions with your community to pass on the thinking behind the analysis produced. Train your community in joint methodologies, search and collaboration facilities, editing, and production of internal reports, comments and dialogues on analysis topics, etc.

Both usage patterns must go on continuously with frequent "updates" and messages to new employees and community participants. No doubt, the first 6 to 12 months require the most effort in this field. Still, even when the information usage capability appears firmly established, ongoing attention is needed from the community manager.

Very early on in our general information usage careers, and then with MCI in particular, we observed very explicit behaviors among people regarding information usage and communication. We labeled this the "Information Carrier Wave" (A term borrowed from radio transmission theory; for every radio channel you tune on your radio, there is an underlying carrier wave with the frequency of the band you tuned in on.) This model has been with us across numerous projects, helping us understand the necessary dynamics of information usage and communication in larger groups.

The "Information Carrier Wave"

Most humans suffer from agoraphobia in one way or another. Since the Stone Age, our genes dictate that we don't stray too far from shelter should a predator show up to threaten us. This fear of uncontrolled exposure seemingly followed us into the communication arena and digital age. Apart from "artists," be it business gurus, movie stars, or theater actors, most individuals dislike public exposure. And even so, these types rarely expose their personal views and opinions, merely playing a role for the audience. Even in today's social media frenzy, most people portray a desired "facade" or personal "brand" rather than their true selves.

Carrying this insight into the business environment of a mid-sized to large company helps us understand the managerial challenge in creating communities that actually perform. Here are two typical examples of management frustration:

"I have a global team of 15 people working with the same account. Why don't they communicate and share information?"

- A qualified guess would be that all have not met physically. Many managers believe the world of social media has reduced the need for actual interaction, but few things could be further from the truth.

- What incentive do they have to share information? Bonuses are probably related to personal rather than team goals—This does not support the community objective!

"We opened a room in MS Teams or Slack so everyone in the organization could share ideas about our work. Why is it still empty after four months?"

- It is a large company! Why would anyone visit your Teams among hundreds of others? What's in it for them? Nothing!

- Talk about agoraphobia! Anyone could find my opinion and use it against me. No way will I take that risk, even though I actually believe I have something to contribute.

The "Information Carrier Wave" is a concept built on the interaction between people management and information management. The traditional way to set up a MCI function is for executive management to introduce procedures for other employees to provide executives with information regarding the competitive environment. In the illustration below, this is labeled the "Dream Line" because of its brilliant appeal to senior management. At first, information begins to feed into the executive office, but it begins to fade again soon. Within less than six months, the pattern usually returns to where it started. Why? Initially, employees feel "honored" when asked to provide C-suite executives with information and a certain glory when blasting an e-mail to the CEO. Soon after though, reality sets in:

- No feedback
- Uncertainty regarding how the information is used
- No incentives to share knowledge

Often, this means the "Dream Line" fades away.

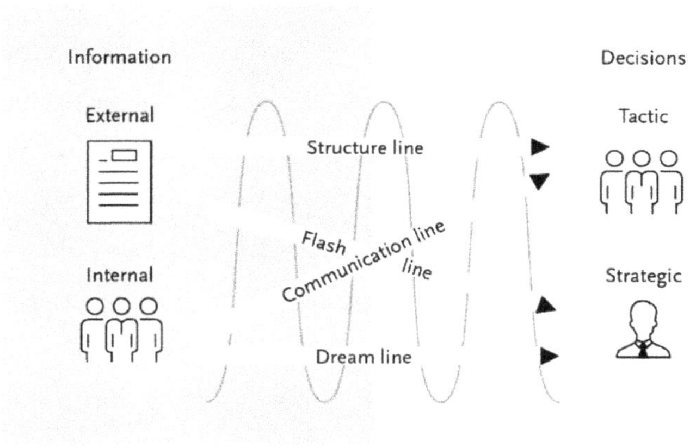

The Information Carrier Wave reduces barriers to knowledge sharing.

To bypass agoraphobia, we find it helps to provide a steady flow of external information whereby each person can comment and add their opinion or insights—this is the Information Carrier Wave. Rather than focusing on executive needs and viewing employees as key transmitters, focus on them as decision-makers and use paid business information sources to perform that role instead.

To bypass agoraphobia, we find it helps to provide a steady flow of external information whereby each person can comment and add their opinion or insights—this is the Information Carrier Wave.

By applying the pre-set classification structure to a significant flow of information from news companies, industry researchers, and financial analysts, we provide a "Structure Line" of information to everyone in the organization. Each little topic in the identified structure will thus have some activity on a daily or weekly basis (akin to "market-making" between financial market brokers). An individual who is part of a team interested in an intelligence topic will now find that news, views, and opinions on such topics are continuously accessible. If he/she decides to take part in the flow, if only by commenting on the external component, this represents a small part of the total picture: with less personal exposure than in the previous situation (the Dream Line concept).

Soon, executive management is made aware of the "structure line" and expects a management summary that we label the "Flash Line", an automated service the MCI team can easily set up.

Last but not least, note that the icons under "Internal Information" and "Tactical Decision" are identical. That is not by chance, as these are the same types of teams. They can be either information *transmitters* or *receivers*. Here we see teams communicate and collaborate on even ground by the "Communication Line"—not "employee to executive." Hence, the perceived risk of "assessment" is significantly smaller. As before, compared to the volume of information in the "carrier wave," each comment or contribution seems insignificant to the individual transmitter. This resembles bees pollinating the entire garden by flying from one flower to the next with the team's help.

However, from a community management perspective, combining such little pieces of information with others comprises the internal information flow that is passed to and from, within and between, company communities. Even if the volume of such rarely exceeds 1-2% of that from the "carrier wave," it remains the 1-2% that will develop into an advantage for the organization as an information asset that competitors cannot copy.

Managing intelligent communities—Human resources

Managing Intelligent Communities differs greatly from regular line management or project management, although its character better resembles the latter overall. The major difference from line management is that Community participants typically do not formally report to the Community manager. The major difference from project management is that a Community is not limited in time (unlike a project). Hence, Community management is about managing people over whom you have no authority for an indefinite time. Challenging is probably the best adjective to describe such a task, yet it is perfectly possible and immensely rewarding from a people management perspective.

Managing an Intelligent Community is really all about key people management skills: incentives, careers, mandates, responsibilities, and all other elements we learn in our line or project management roles. However, the major difference is that in line and project management roles, you tend to be assigned coworkers while they are assigned to you as a manager. It's true that in the hiring process, there is clearly an element of the potential recruit choosing between you and other suitors with competing offers. That aside, after employees join the organization, the possibility of refusing a reorganization or particular project assignment is limited. Once, maybe, but twice in a row—no, then you are labeled a troublemaker. As a community manager, however, you are continuously on the recruiting track. Participants choose you, not the other way around. Of course, you do have some ability to refuse participation, but even that is challenging in most cases.

Hence, key management issues are attracting, inspiring, and offering alternative career paths and making it likely that certain benefits will come with it by joining this particular community. For a community manager to do this, he/she must be well-acquainted with company culture. Many issues must be addressed as enablers in the organization rather than direct incentives for community members. One example is that of career paths. The fact that the community manager has no immediate responsibility over community members immediately rules out his/her direct impact on participant job descriptions. Rather, the community manager must "sell" the virtues of the community's competence-development and experience-building components to general management so they will automatically consider one of your community members for promotion to a senior role.

The "attraction component" is built in many ways, but recognize two key characteristics of individual choice:

- Will this help me do my current job better?
- Will I learn something new?

Unless the answer to both of these questions is yes, the community manager will most likely fail to keep the community operating. Create the "do my current job better" factor through value-added networking aspects. "The more I put into the community, the more I get out of it, by a factor of 5 to 10."

The learning aspect requires two specific actions from the community manager—training and challenging tasks:

- Training is, and will always be, at the core of community building and management. The community manager's responsibility is to ensure that advanced training programs, which keep community participants abreast of decision-makers within their field of specialization, are available in-house or through outsourced activities. It should include agreed-upon methodologies (see below), standard business analysis knowledge, and intra-company understanding.

- To achieve continuous learning, one must also ensure tasks addressed by the community reach and extend beyond a certain level of complexity. A community that frequently deals with simple tasks will not attract those you are seeking. The key measure is to help decision-makers trust community competence and require more advanced output.

The importance of transparent strategy communication cannot be overly stressed so that everyone in the organization is aware of key group strategy aspects. Unless that is the case, community work will lack a decision framework to base their analysis, recommendations, and operations. It is the community manager's responsibility to ensure the strategy is available to all participants.

Last but not least, it is the community manager's duty to enable participants to physically meet to develop rapport and foster communication. Network meetings, annual or quarterly seminars, project work, and development meetings are varied formats to use for such a purpose. Just keep in mind that this must produce tangible outputs to avoid the label of fringe travel benefits!

The positive effects of working Intelligent Communities are many, but one in particular when addressing MCI is market perception.

Intelligent communities as information receptors

Most of our discussion has so far focused on how to make communities cross-communicate and share results with given decision-maker constituencies. However, one of the most valuable capabilities of a working intelligent community is information gathering. As we prefer to call it, information *reception*—as it should reflect an ongoing radar antenna that never turns off.

Utilizing your community as a global radar for business events and developments is not such a complex task. "All" you must do is ensure the community is heavily involved in both strategy making and future analysis by, for example, participating in scenario workshops (see Chapter 10). By actually being part of the development process, the community at large will view the information flow and human contacts outside of the organization as continuous verifiers or falsifiers of the current agreed-upon strategic picture. By using those insights in community communication, internal information flow, and input for changes to information needs and structure definitions, one will eventually create a "self-tuning" surveillance system to stay ahead of the competition.

Managing intelligent communities—Methodologies

To build a successful community, you should deploy a set of shared methodologies as standard working models and ensure all community members apply them to their daily work. The key is to help the community develop a common language.

Although information is the key nutrient for any Intelligent Community, its people are its core. The major challenge in managing Intelligent Communities is not an IT system but the operations aspect of keeping the community inspired and proactive. To build a successful community, deploy a set of shared methodologies as standard working models and ensure all community members apply them to their daily work. The key is to help the community develop a common language. No, we are not referring to English or any other national language, but rather a matter of agreeing on analysis word definitions and the like. For example, consider the words "strategy," "marketing," and "positioning." Any MCI analyst knows the list of concepts that can lead to misunderstandings is endless. Still, this must be addressed within a community before it can truly operate (as part of the training mentioned above). The key is to understand the methodologies that will enable faster and more precise communication and collaborative work. Whether we choose the most modern, advanced, and complex analytics models or simply a good old SWOT is irrelevant. More often than not, the latter is better because it is much faster to deploy. Still, even the term "SWOT" can mean different things to different people, not always leading to the same goals.

As soon as the community agrees on the methodologies to deploy and term definitions therein, the immediate next question concerns the related work mode, communication, and analysis. By sheer experience, the only answer here is templates.

Many perceive templates as belonging to the old bureaucratic world and believe they have no place in modern business. On the contrary, templates are here to stay. They are important and must reflect business maker needs. Used correctly, templates help make communication faster, more efficient, and even of higher quality.

As an example, take the simplest base for corporate strategy making: reports from all countries in which you operate. Imagine they all look identical and use the same economic figures background (EIU, IMF, OECD, or UN…but ONE of them) to make forecasts, analytical methods, and chapter structure comparable to produce parallel insights and enable proper prioritization and corporate resource deployment plans. Furthermore, imagine these reports are not static/updated once a year, but rather dynamic documents continuously updated by community individuals in each country. Your intelligent community will in turn build a near real-time strategy "trading system" for all decision-makers, contributing significant value by its sheer comparability, cross recognizability, and information rapidity.

With respect to competitor studies, account/customer analysis, procurement/supplier management, etc., the template structure's value to otherwise unstructured information is immense! Quite obviously, such templates fundamentally follow an identical structure to related needs and taxonomies.

Taking this one step further, community participants can now easily identify each other and enjoy a common way to communicate proactively. Each key monitoring topic (e.g., country, customer, competitor, and product) should have its own designated MCI analyst responsible for covering his/her particular topic. Such analysts are very rarely full-time and typically reflect a combination of job descriptions, such as account management, strategy, development, or marketing. With an Intelligent Community like this in place, the monetary and efficiency rewards are enormous.

Using incentives to encourage participants

An Intelligent Community does not just appear by itself—it must be built. Participants should be selected by considering several variables, including experience, mandates, network, geography, and any other qualification that might add value to this particular community. Perhaps the worst mistake is to assign a line unit as a community node and hope this transforms into "community thinking." No value-added would be created in this way. The value comes from different individuals with different perspectives! Hence, it takes time to develop a powerful community.

Also, as Intelligent Community work is grounded in communication and information sharing rather than line or project management mandates, the concept of incentives must be afforded attention. Why would people just want to share information? After all, information is both power and value. Almost every MCI manager, HR manager, and IT manager we have spoken with echoes the same concern and frustration; "No matter which incentive system I apply, it gets misused."

Consider the following examples of incentive challenges:

- Incentive: "For each piece of information you report, we will reward you with a dollar or check!"

Response: Information starts to flood in! It is all unstructured, and 98% is useless. Furthermore, a full-time employee is needed to find the 2% that is useful.

- Incentive: "For every *useful* piece of information you report, we will reward you with a dollar or check!"

Response: Who determines the usefulness? As the judge, you will soon lose your popularity as the manager of this system!

- Incentive: "At the end of each month, we will log whose reports have been downloaded the most, and the top 10 people will be rewarded!"

Response: "If I download your files this month, you download my files next month, OK?"

First and foremost, "There is no such thing as a free lunch." An organization that succeeds in encouraging their employees to undertake activities with 100% altruistic motivations and no personal benefits attached does not exist. However, the benefits need not be monetary and not necessarily immediate. One "incentive system" that almost always works is to continuously add value to your CV, for internal and external use. In 1994 (and a bit ahead of his time), London Business School Dean George Bain said, "No MBA graduate will accept a job offer in the future unless the employer can prove that the position will add at least one significant value item to the CV each and every six months."

Applying this thinking to any community in an organization really means to embed community thinking into the core of career planning and management. If one succeeds in building into a culture the notion that "If I produce business value through altruistic community work in this position, I will be considered for a higher pay/more advanced/better status position very soon," participating in advanced communities will become an incentive in itself.

Key takeaways

Summarizing the key takeaways of this chapter:

- An Intelligent Community is a network of trained knowledge workers who systematically work together to maximize the value of their combined knowledge.

- In an Intelligent Community, members choose whether to participate or not, and the community manager's only recruitment tool is the attraction of the community itself.

- Keep human behavior at heart! A community is built on a combination of trust, altruism, and incentives and must be cultivated and managed accordingly.

- To bypass agoraphobia, we find it helps to provide a steady flow of external information whereby each person can comment and add their opinion or insights—this is the Information Carrier Wave.

- The modus operandi is key to success. Unless entirely transparent and unanimous, community efficiency will suffer significantly and may cause the initiative to fade away.

CHAPTER 10

How to Prepare People for Change and Disruption

We are approaching the end of this part of the book. If everything mentioned previously is already present within your organization, congrats! You are working for an insightful, forward-looking company. Still, there is one thing we have so far only addressed as an overreaching goal: the capability of foresight. How can you affix your own crystal ball and see into the future? No, we don't really believe crystal ball-like capabilities exist. Still, it is perfectly possible to be "future-ready" and rapidly prepare for change and disruptions in the business environment. In this final chapter of "Digging Deeper," we introduce some working methods that will help do just that. It will inspire you with suggested models, each one having the capacity to fill a textbook with theories and guidelines. Still, introducing one or more of these will inevitably prepare people for change and disruption.

With a complete MCI function in place, you will transform your organization into a huge team of "**Intelligence**

Seekers" (or Observers), building a second-to-none "**Understanding Mechanism.**" This is an embedded capability for insights that enables the entire organization to understand and manage operations in line with market risks, expectations, and opportunities. So, now what?

The magic word is spelled F-O-R-E-S-I-G-H-T, and the key executive capability to achieve is to Never be Surprised.

At this point in development, many organizations tend to get comfortable and bask in the immediate support it lends shorter-term marketing, sales planning, product mix and pricing strategy goals, and long-term planning for strategy and positioning. Granted, if just fractions of these application areas fully employ the investment's new capabilities, this will contribute a positive return. Still, why not make the most of a now fully-developed operational capability that is ripe for further utilization? The magic word is spelled **F-O-R-E-S-I-G-H-T**, and the key executive capability to achieve is to **Never be Surprised**.

Preparing for the future is usually a corporate management task that, in all honesty, is not always at the top of the agenda. Instead, short-term matters tend to become the top priority. Even though companies' public communications often seek to portray corporate strategy as a deeply analyzed and thought-through series of actions, it is a well-known fact that "gut feelings" often influence more long-term decisions. There are two main reasons for this:

a) Highly experienced and competent industry leaders have the credibility to act on gut feelings—some truly thrive on this. Still, this is a high-risk strategy if the executive board is forced to place all their trust in the CEO's intuition.

b) A lack of alternatives often exists—very few organizations have institutionalized foresight management and analysis processes in place, and no CEO or corporate strategist wishes to hire a team of management consultants every time the horizon looks beyond twelve months ahead.

With an established MCI operation, the game plan changes completely. In preparing for market changes, disruptions, technology leaps, or other business environment developments, corporate and regional management can now access a wealth of insights and market/business information to address future-oriented matters.

When the future knocks on the door, it never walks away.

The future has a tendency to appear by surprise, and the key to success is to plan in advance and thus not *be* surprised. When the future knocks on the door, it never walks away. The concrete results of such preparedness are an ability to survive transitions, construct a proactive patent portfolio, and employ forward-looking M&A strategies such as more surgical/future-oriented positioning, targeted capex investments, and cost-effective capabilities, just to name a few. Also, an oft-referred to "side effect" of such programs is the branding impact of thought leadership industry perceptions. In some cases, companies with the most powerful and thought-through foresight can steer market development in the direction of their own plans and thereby reap further financial gains from future planning.

The challenge management faces in seeking to uncover these benefits is to simply "ask the right questions." Analyzing the future is not the same as producing forecasts. Rather, it is to "paint pictures" of potential tomorrows and prepare a range of "what if?" responses based on these pictures, ready for immediate deployment when Future X knocks on the door. A range of analytics tools and/or activities support both question formation and picture painting phases. Still, a common denominator is the massive use of MCI input. Thus, again, as your MCI capabilities are already established and the most complicated challenge to overcome is thereby dismantled, it would be almost misconduct not to initiate a structured foresights analysis for executive management.

As stated in the chapter introduction, we present here by no means even introductory texts on future-analytics tools but merely inspiration for further reading on varied working models at hand.

Within the MCI networks, the competence to undertake this analysis must be found and supporting insights and information reside within the same domain. Hence, for corporate and regional management, it is merely a matter of assigning the task of "senior executive foresight management" to corporate MCI management and also ensure ongoing, transparent dialogue with (and reporting from) MCI with this particular focus. The additional resource requirements are marginal while long-term business effects are significant: a cost-benefit calculation with only one possible outcome.

On a personal note from us authors, for a MCI manager, this is among the most interesting, rewarding, and flat-out fun analytics areas to work with—so fingers crossed that your organization gives it a go.

Let's start preparing your organization for the future! Here are some of the most common foresight tools that can use Market and Competitive Intelligence as a foundation:

- Scenario planning
- Business war games
- Trend radars
- Early warning systems
- Innovation management

Scenario planning

Theories for scenario analysis are many, and different techniques are preferred for different applications. Common factors include trend clustering analytics, forcing managers and analysts to articulate critical development factors and link them with internal resource and capability development. Scenario Analysis is indisputably one of the most powerful foresight management tools available, but it requires a significant number of resources.

While working with scenario planning, participants begin to see the business environment from new perspectives. The trends and "what ifs" tend to include factors that are not immediately adjacent to the day-to-day business, meaning those involved will develop a sense of seeing important event signals that, for others, are neutral and unrelated to current business.

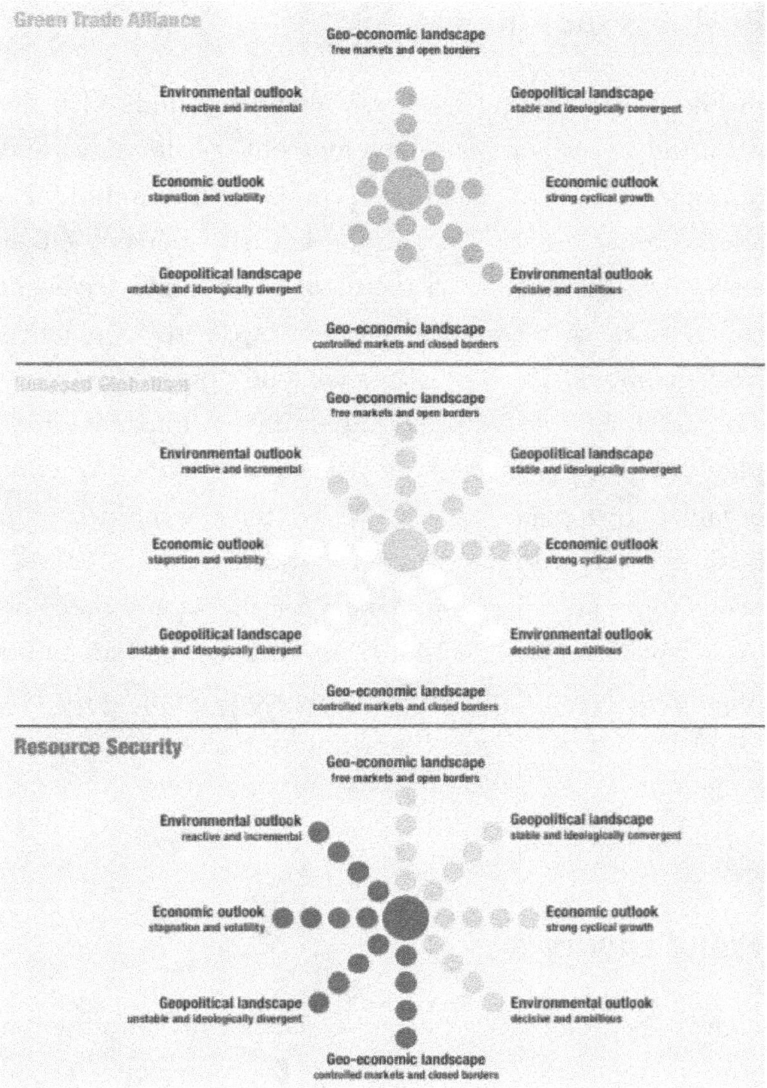

Mining and Metals Scenarios to 2030
(Source: World Economic Forum).

Business war games

Business war gaming is exactly what it sounds like: the gamification of strategic development, positioning, and resource utilization. The basic premise is that individuals adopt strategic roles for various industry players: either customers, competitors, regulators, or other relevant counterparts that can either amplify or destroy a planned strategic move. The key is to enable all "players" to truly embrace their role by providing sufficient information to play up opportunities or severe threats to your organization's plans (e.g., as "CEO of the key competitor"). Business wargames are a main working method for MCI teams to prepare decision-makers for almost any outcome of a given set of decisions—serving as an advanced hypothesis-testing procedure. Time-consuming, yes, but for plans and decisions with significant economic impacts on the line, it is worth every minute.

Trend radars

Trend Radars is a collective label for information management models and tools that correlate actual developments with management-assumed trends and "notifies" on discrepancies between hypothesis and reality. This is particularly powerful support for Scenario

Analysis, but it can also work on a stand-alone basis for long-term Key Intelligence Topic analysis.

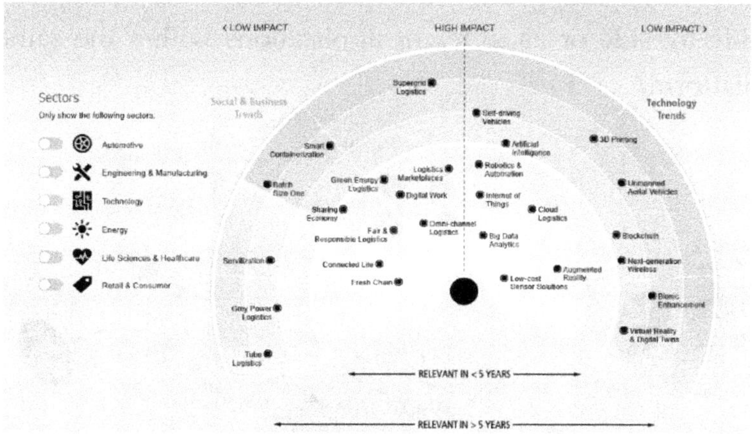

DHL's Logistics Trend Radar (Source: DHL website, https://www.dhl.com/global-en/home/insights-and-innovation/insights/logistics-trend-radar.html).

Trend radars have the benefit of rather "easy" implementation within MCI platforms, and as such, gain wide visibility throughout an organization. Also, many individuals are inspired to follow trends and discuss potential "future tomorrows," so a trend radar helps enable organization-wide future-readiness.

Early Warning (EW) systems

EW platforms are quite the opposite of Trend Radars. If a Trend Radar deviates from what is assumed, EW platforms try to alert users on matters they have not considered but still impact business foresight. It is usually advisable to work with Trend Radars and EW platforms side by side or as different applications within the same platform.

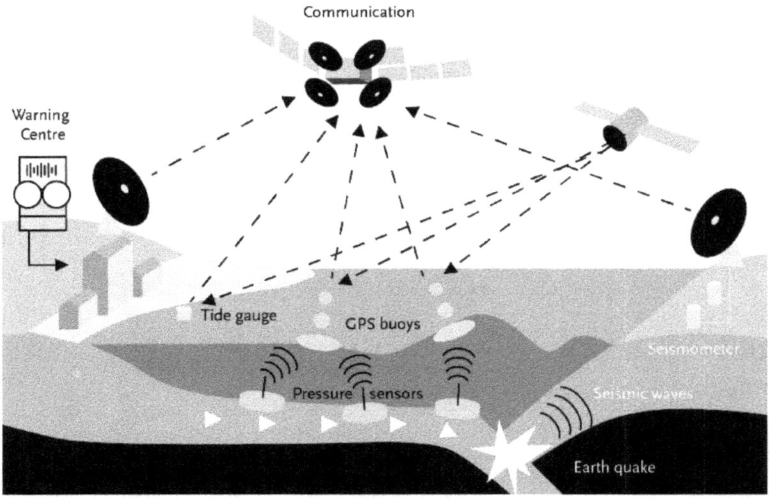

***Early Warning System for Tsunamis in the Indian Ocean (Source:* "The challenge of installing a tsunami early warning system in the vicinity of the Sunda Arc, Indonesia", by Lauterjung, Muench, Rudloff, Natural Hazards and Earth System Science, Vol 10, 6 April, 2010).**

An EW component of an MCI platform is more for target groups of managers and analysts. The outputs are more often than not rather "weak signals" that require interpretation, and in the wrong communication channels, may only cause confusion or stir up unnecessary concern. However, for analysts and management layers, an EW system can sometimes serve as a make-or-break matter when preparing for both significant opportunities and major threats.

Innovation management

Innovation, or simply coming up with new ideas for service, product or operations development, is key to growth and long-term survival. A company that does not innovate will soon find itself without market relevance and slowly decay. Innovation is far too often perceived as something that "just happens." Still, the truth is that management can enable and spur innovation in very structured ways—it cannot be planned but definitely managed. In the context of MCI, it is a matter of providing employees with access to both education and challenging information alongside work tasks that enable them to synthesize new insights: thereby possibly seeing gaps to fill and opportunities to grab more quickly than competitors. For that purpose, the tools above can serve as sources of inspiration, but the innovation process itself needs its own approach—which is why we address it with this short overview.

Key takeaways

Summarizing the key takeaways of this chapter:

- The future tends to strike by surprise, but MCI boasts tools to mitigate the effects.
- We describe some of the most common foresight tools that can use Market and Competitive Intelligence as a foundation, namely:
    - Scenario planning
    - Business war games
    - Trend radars
    - Early warning systems
    - Innovation management
- Change and disruption can be tremendously costly. Although the words bear negative connotation for most, it can represent true opportunities for those who are prepared.
- Working models for future preparedness are many. Find those most suitable for your particular organization and culture.

PART IV

Beyond the Garden Walls

The final, fourth, part answers the **"Now what?"** question, i.e. what do you do with all your insights? Anyone who has attempted to develop a beautiful and long-lasting garden know that you cannot relax just because your first rhododendrons are blooming and you have harvested your first sweet oranges. A garden needs constant attention and influences from the outside will be critical. Chapter 11 to 13 are there to provide a future perspective and inspiration.

CHAPTER 11

Becoming a Healthier Organization

Gardens are built for specific purposes and are often historically surrounded by comparably high walls. The obvious reason for this is to protect the produce and beauty from theft and demolition and shield crops from severe weather. Perhaps less well-known is that regular walls, without any roofing, contribute to a higher ground temperature that enables faster plant growth inside the wall than outside. The temperature difference can rise by three degrees, a huge difference when aiming for early spring vegetables.

When developing a MCI operation and establishing teams, people-networks, external collaborations, and community operations really do resemble those in the garden. Trust and rapid initiated dialogue and communication develop quickly based on agreed forms and models. Moreover, the culture within a large intelligent community will often feel both rewarding and comfortable for members. In short, the environment inside the garden of intelligence walls is perfect for cultivating sought-after insights.

Still, we must not forget that the ultimate aim is to ensure the fruits of the garden are truly beneficial for those who contribute to and consume garden insights results. If you invest time and resources to grow a garden, you, of course, seek a return on this investment.

MCI is a strategic capability that is implemented to gain a competitive advantage in turbulent business environments. That is all very well said and done, but what does it mean? Are there more concrete benefits to strive for? The answer is yes.

MCI returns can be described as five different "health areas" of an organization:

1. Healthier Decisions
2. Healthier Market Position
3. Healthier Ways of Working
4. Healthier Financials
5. Healthier Future

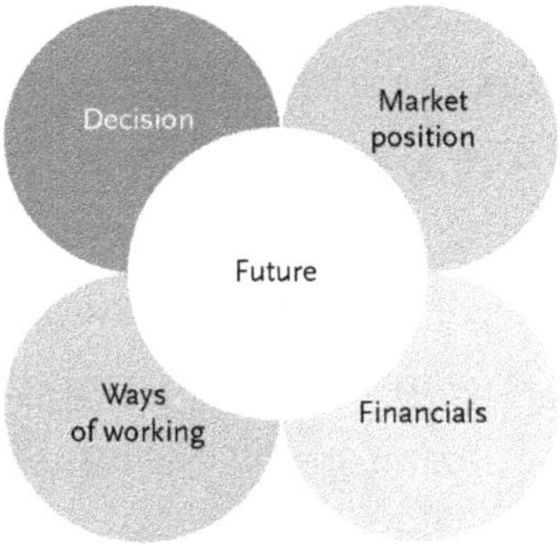

MCI leads to a healthier organization across five areas.

Healthier decisions

Making better decisions is perhaps the primary justification for MCI as a key component for company success. The challenge is that many seem to believe only senior executives make important decisions. Imagine if you could sum up the economic value of every single organizational decision and then compare the executive part with the accumulated value of 99% of all others. Yes, the immediate value of those would by far exceed the value of executive choices. Having said that, executive decisions can be of tremendous strategic value in that they set the entire operation on course, but the point is not to forget the ongoing daily decision-making by every single employee. Here, MCI helps big time! One could take this so far as to say that MCI is essentially a decision-support service.

MCI is essentially a decision-support service.

MCI contributes with the following three decision benefits:

1. **Better basis for decisions**: By significantly reducing the risk of failure and increasing the chance to seize business opportunities

2. **Faster decisions**: By shortening the time to insights, MCI enables faster decisions and quicker response times to market events

3. **Improved decision understanding**: This is the capability to build structural experiences from decisions made. When a decision is shown to be wrong (yes, this will still happen, even with MCI), the ability to trace the grounds for that decision will make it far easier to rapidly review, understand, and change if time permits, also learning for future decisions.

Healthier market position

One key strategic area for all companies is that of market positioning. That is, the work to manage the market *perception* of the offering in relation to the competition. This goes hand in hand with company branding and communication of brand values to mirror the sentiments of the target market. MCI can contribute massively by tracking market sentiments on a granular level, geography-wise, product/service-wise, and thereby craft marketing communications and competitive positioning.

MCI will contribute with the following three market position benefits:

1. **Improved listening ability**. MCI is the most advanced "market listening tool" an organization has. Listen to the market, customers, and competitors and tune your message accordingly.

2. **Competitor benchmarking.** MCI will improve your ability to differentiate yourself versus your competitors. This will help you showcase your strengths and advantages and help you win deals.

3. **Focused customer targeting**. With the help of MCI, your marketing messages can be clearer and more focused towards your most suitable customer segments.

Healthier ways of working

Organizations face many challenges, and MCI can obviously not solve all of them. Yet, it *can* help eliminate one of the most tricky organizational concerns: suboptimal human resources and isolation frustration.

Our experience is that the overwhelming majority of employees want to do a good job. We do not buy into statements like, "Most go to work just to get paid and then go home again." As individuals, *we want to succeed* and be allowed to feel good about that. Each success can be very small on an individual and daily basis, but the individual employee thrives on it. Often, frustrations build upon feelings of a lack of involvement, not understanding how to fit into the overall operation or if others are performing similar tasks faster and better. Management often underestimates the human requirement to understand one's surroundings to feel safe and needed as part of a group.

Where does MCI fit into this perspective? Belonging and involvement! A MCI platform can do wonders for individuals in an organization simply to understand company strategy or "the big picture," and how both the organization and employee fit into that accordingly. It is also highly likely that employees set out to contribute to MCI efforts as observers of the market.

MCI will contribute with the following two organizational benefits:

1. **Productivity gains**: due to reduced misunderstandings/double work as a common foundation for business discussions

2. **Increased innovation**: as people get more involved and see/relate to company strategy, unleashing a creative force that often drives innovation

Heathier financials

We must obviously address how MCI leads to financial benefits, expressed in positive changes in either (or both) of the organization's Profit and Loss (P&L) or balance sheet statement.

Starting with the P&L and **cost** part of that, we should recognize that MCI *is* a cost-cutting measure in itself. The challenge is often proving "MCI costs" for the organization before the actual MCI program is set into place. Yet, two factors usually suffice to calculate cost savings:

1. The amount spent on commercial content tends to exceed that of centralized procurement of the same material by a large factor. This is also easy to calculate and prove.

2. The time spent by all decision-makers and staff to search for information supporting their decisions. Assume you can save only 10% of that time with MCI system support, and the cost savings will be very apparent.

MCI's contribution to **revenue** generation is harder to "prove," but an accepted estimate involves assuming it contributes an insight solely responsible for securing a new customer contract win. What is MCI worth in that particular moment in time? Answer: exactly the gross margin of the contract. Real-life is, of course, never as black and white as this example, but in some cases, sounds like: *"We knew this before the competition did, in turn positioning us more favorably in front of the customer as we look to win the contract."* This is a "real-life" statement shared multiple times by account managers inquiring about MCI benefits. Just like in marketing efforts, measurement is tricky, but the benefit still exists. Add up some of these gross margins, and you will find that merely a fraction is enough to warrant MCI funding.

The link between MCI and **balance sheet** items is less obvious. Yet, it exists, and we must apply a risk management perspective of MCI here. Balance sheet items that can benefit significantly from MCI insights are actual and planned receivables and evaluation of goodwill. Both can function to review the viability of businesses considered account assets, for which potential and sudden failures can kill results and company equity. This is typically not a standard MCI service, but it is worth suggesting to the CFO as a possibility. MCI will contribute with the following four financial benefits:

1. **Reduced costs of information sources**—thanks to centralized and coordinated procurement

2. **Reallocated cost of staff**—thanks to time savings in decision processes

3. **Increased gross margin**—thanks to additional contracts won by sales

4. **Reduced risk**—thanks to lower risk on the balance sheet (goodwill and receivables)

Healthier future

If there is one benefit we are fully convinced of, it's MCI's ability to keep organizations fit and prepared for any challenges and disruptions that may appear in the future. But to do this, you must sometimes use your persuasive skills to convince decision-makers to consume your produce, because not everyone likes all the fruits and vegetables coming from the garden. In modern terminology, MCI professionals should think of themselves as influencers or personal trainers of decision-makers. If you are in good shape, you will have more strength to withstand any storms, diseases, difficulties, crises, or challenges that come your way.

MCI professionals should think of themselves as influencers or personal trainers of decision-makers.

We have concluded that focus shifts from traditional competitor monitoring toward discovering and developing new markets and customers, and perhaps even completely new business models—an even more future-oriented approach. Each shock to the system induces change, and

Covid-19 is certainly no exception to that rule. Hence, MCI will play an even more important role going forward.

In any crisis or disruptive situation, most decision-makers focus on the immediate here and now, often in firefighting mode. This leaves little time to plan for the future, which means this is another role that MCI professionals will take on: helping their organizations plan for and prepare for the post-disruption world. MCI focuses on detecting weak signals of prosperous ideas within this realm. What are the early warning signals from suppliers, competitors, customers, and market developments?

Furthermore, there is a clear "What If?" aspect to the disruption preparedness discussed here, which is in itself a key input for more elaborate risk assessment or analysis. This is not everyone's favorite thing to work, often falling into the category of "I know we should do this, but there are too many other urgent things today." Amid disruption or crisis, MCI tools and knowledge can help. MCI will contribute with the following two future fitness benefits:

- **More agility.** MCI will provide a more agile and flexible organization that can quickly adapt to changes in the environment and strategic direction of the organization.
- **Higher growth.** MCI will prepare the organization to address future threats and opportunities.

Measuring the value

Given the value an MCI platform has to an organization, it is vital for success to measure this value as accurately as possible. We strongly recommend using a set of Key Performance Indicators (KPI) to measure the progress of your MCI platform, because what is not measured doesn't get done. KPIs are a more forward-looking predictor of MCI performance than e.g. more financially based Return on Investment (ROI) calculations.

By defining and monitoring the right KPIs, you can gain valuable insight into your operations and make the adjustments needed to optimize your performance. The challenge is knowing which KPIs are most important to monitor to get the results you want. MCI involves trying to measure the intangible, a bit like trying to measure the effects of marketing. To do this, you must consider a mix of both more objective, quantitative and more subjective, qualitative performance indicators.

Our recommendation is to define the metrics that matter most to your organization, both hard & soft. Intelligence teams vary greatly in maturity and ambition levels, which means that you need to carefully consider the purpose and application of your MCI platform. Not all companies are alike and not all metrics fit into a standardized box, so spend time early in the start of your project to determine your specific goals and associated metrics.

Continually evaluate, review and analyze your KPI's as they may change and evolve over time.

Hard, quantitative indicators	**Soft, qualitative indicators**
Usage Statistics: • No. of users, total • No. of active (logged in users per week/month) • No. of daily email alerts • No. of search queries	User satisfaction surveys Interviews with core users Quality and freshness of intelligence
Output, Deliverables • No. of requests (demand) • Response time • Estimate time spent on research versus analysis • No. of reports produced	Knowledge sharing culture Level of involvement in decision making processes Strategic awareness in organization
Cost savings by centralizing information	Win/Loss analysis on deals where CI has been involved

Table: Examples of hard and soft Key Performance Indicators (KPIs) for MCI.

The most important thing is perhaps not exactly which KPIs you select, but to make sure to measure the ones you have selected consistently over time and to publish the results widely. Don't just use them to justify the investment, but also to improve your MCI tools and systems.

Key takeaways

Summarizing the key takeaways of this chapter:

- MCI strengthens the competitive advantages of any organization by providing:
  - Healthier Decisions
  - Healthier Market Position
  - Healthier Ways of Working
  - Healthier Financials
  - Healthier Future
- To prove the value of MCI, it must be measured. MCI has concrete and measurable benefits that are universally applicable. They depend on the purpose of MCI. Find those most relevant to your organization.

- Fundamentally, MCI is a decision-support service for the entire organization. It is through these decisions that health will prosper.

- Define and use Key Performance Indicators (KPIs) to measure the value of MCI in your organization.

CHAPTER 12

Inspirational Cases

When embarking on a project like building a Garden of Intelligence, every now and then, one tends to face some type of "organizational identity crises," and a range of "anxiety questions" arise:

- What are we really doing?
- This was complicated; are we the only ones experiencing this?
- Now, what was the purpose again? Can anyone recall?

No, you are not alone! Yes, others have experienced similar situations! It is perfectly normal sometimes to lose sight of a long-term goal, particularly if the situation is for any reason temporarily not ideal. The seven cases illustrated in this chapter are simply for inspirational purposes. All of them are real-life examples that are anonymized in some cases.

1. **Information-related case:** How a manufacturing company improves consistency and quality with MCI
2. **Information-related case:** How a global technology company gathers all intelligence sources in one place
3. **Technology-related case:** How the Intelligence2day® platform supports MCI
4. **Technology-related case:** How Netflix uses Machine Learning to guide users to the most relevant content
5. **Technology-related case:** How a legal firm achieved enterprise value from its Intelligence Platform
6. **People-related case:** How Ericsson turned its workforce into Intelligence Gatherers
7. **People-related case:** How an energy company tracks future scenarios

INFORMATION CASE: How a manufacturing company improves consistency and quality with MCI

This is a case study about an international technology manufacturer with approximately 15,000 employees and multiple information centers that serve parts of the organization related to varied sectors in which they have product portfolios.

The need

Each company information center had a different solution to track market intelligence, some of which were in-house solutions. Since there was no cooperation or communication between these systems, a steering committee formed to select one product to use across the entire corporation.

The solution

After a thorough evaluation process, the organization selected a MCI platform that is now successfully used across the corporation. Each of the four information centers utilizing the platform has its own market intelligence sources—in total, 1,300 different feeds are established throughout the system. Big competitors and industry topics are covered through intelligence provided by the organization's licensed news provider. However, it's important to note that not everything can be found in licensed sources.

For example, one center's competitive landscape is heavily weighted towards small private companies that cannot be effectively tracked through licensed sources. To capture information about these competitors, the information center set up RSS feeds for new information on these private company websites and Google alerts for competitors/specified topics.

While running a pilot program, the information centers implemented content feeds, tweaked system settings, and troubleshot software upgrades. Now that the system is up and running, the only thing that consistently takes time to maintain is finding and fixing broken website links.

One challenge they face is deciphering how to get better information about markets in China and Japan. News monitoring in these languages is complex, and company websites seem to change constantly, requiring the information centers to update their feed settings.

Possessing only one corporate-wide intelligence system has resulted in great cost savings. By centralizing intelligence work, a high level of consistency and quality is maintained across the entire organization. The company now has a good overview of all company intelligence—

what information they have and where it is located. Also, varied information centers can easily communicate and cooperate with each other and avoid duplicate work.

Content tip!

Information centers at this company recommend reviewing three factors when examining potential content sources:

- **Right content:** Consider sources from which you can draw the best content. If you consistently need intelligence from licensed sources, you will need to pay accordingly, but there are several situations wherein licensed sources will not offer what you need. For example, if videos and images are required for your content, these are only available from public sources. If your competitors are privately-held companies, licensed sources will probably not deliver the desired content.

- **Cost:** Consider the financial implications of employing free sources versus licensed sources.

- **Efficiency:** Using free sources is not as efficient as using licensed sources. While the latter delivers full article text to the platform, the former only pulls in a few sentences; hence, you will have to copy-paste the full article text on a manual basis.

INFORMATION CASE: How a global technology company gathers all intelligence sources in one place

The information center at a large global technology company used an in-house solution to track market intelligence from hundreds of sources across various sectors. However, in 2015, they found it was not meeting the needs of users, who sought an improved way to search amongst these sources and the ability to receive e-mail alerts for relevant content. They thus wanted an intelligence system that could accommodate social features, such as the ability to "like" and comment on content.

The team incorporated three types of content into their new system:

- Reports from licensed research vendors
- News from premium business sources
- Internally produced material

One employee, known as the information manager, is responsible for keeping the system running optimally, including:

- Evaluating sources
- Creating feeds
- Uploading content manually
- Troubleshooting

- Working with vendors to create FTP and API import mechanisms
- Negotiating content licenses

The information manager speaks with approximately 25 of their 165 content vendors weekly and an additional 15 vendors monthly. Moreover, the manager maintains a quarterly scorecard—a report of the content type and volume the vendor has delivered over the quarter and its usefulness for users.

With all information sources automatically gathered into one single platform, users now have a quick and easy way to find what they are looking for. If any new relevant information comes in or someone comments on or "likes" a particular article, they will receive an e-mail notification to ensure they don't miss anything important.

The information manager also conducts annual surveys that ask users to rate the types of content they use in their jobs. While these efforts are time-consuming, they produce these benefits:

- Knowing whether a content source is performing consistently. If not, they investigate whether they need to troubleshoot for a technical issue or whether the content is no longer valuable to the business.

- Reinforcing confidence in the value of each vendor's content, which allows for data-driven budgeting decisions and advocacy as well as a position of strength in negotiations.

Content tip!

- The information manager suggests paying close attention to the negotiation and documentation of licensing terms for each piece of content.

- These terms are a critical element of copyright-related risk management. Recommendations include paying for two or three sources with terms that enable users to use and share content in a widespread manner and allocating extra funds for departmental or global licensing rather than city-based licensing.

- Ultimately, it is more time- and cost-efficient to have confidence about widespread use than it is to track down licensing agreements for many disparate pieces of content (or for how that content can be used in different locations).

TECHNOLOGY CASE: How the Intelligence2day® platform supports MCI

An example of a MCI platform many organizations use is Intelligence2day[13], a cloud-based software platform developed and provided by Comintelli.

Intelligence2day® is an insight engine for Market and Competitive Intelligence. It automatically collects, discovers, organizes, analyzes, and shares information and knowledge. Intelligence2day® focuses on any aspect of the competitive landscape (e.g., customers, competitors, products, markets, technologies, and trends).

There are many ways to define and redefine intelligence projects using Intelligence2day®. For example, Heat Maps, Trending Themes, and Signal Spotter can be used. A company that works with automated production solutions leveraging an IoT (Internet of Things) might use the Heat Map below to discuss the need to start monitoring the Food and Beverage industry in Asia.

---

[13] Source: www.intelligence2day.com.

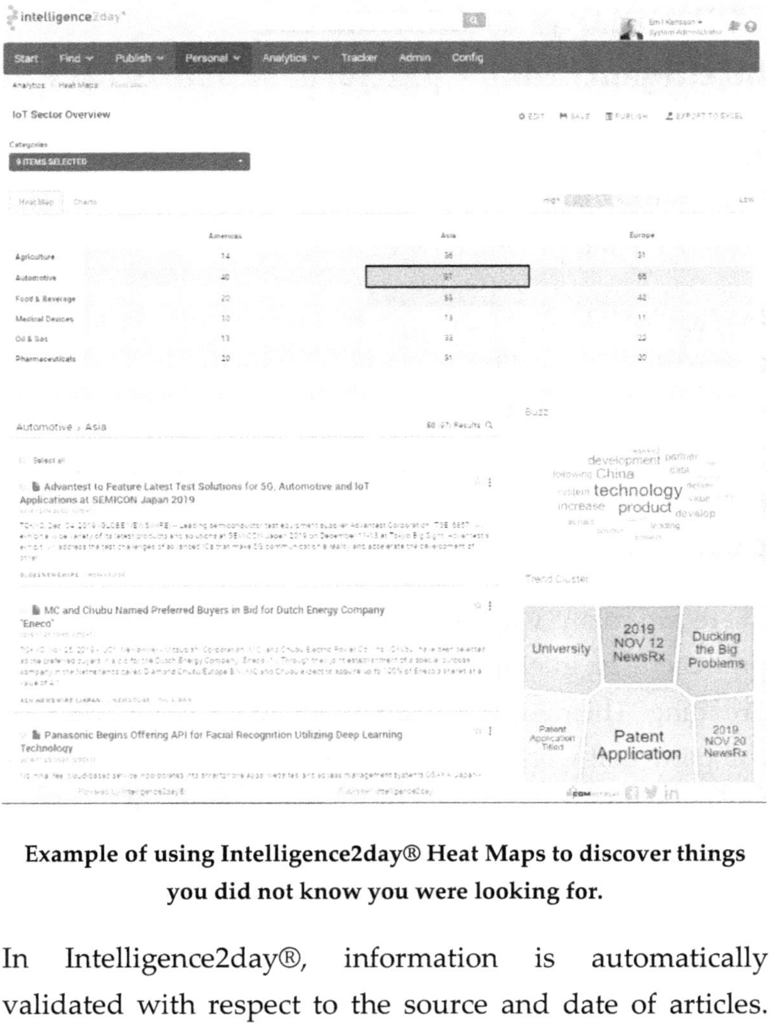

Example of using Intelligence2day® Heat Maps to discover things you did not know you were looking for.

In Intelligence2day®, information is automatically validated with respect to the source and date of articles. Colleagues can also comment on content to inform others on how valuable it is, etc. Content can also be flagged and tagged in varied ways to validate content.

Intelligence2day® report generation is flexible and suits an organization's unique intelligence needs. Set up is quick, with automatic content generation and assigned groups for distribution. There are also different profile templates to choose from. Profile templates are easily customized for particular intelligence needs. Content can be uploaded and shared from external applications and drives.

In Intelligence2day®, the reach can be extended by reusing and customizing published content for different audiences. For instance, a report on a specific market trend might include articles related to a specific competitor—that information that can be reused in a competitor analysis report. Reports can be shared and discussed among these audience across many different channels: within the tool itself, of course, or external platforms like e-mail, Salesforce, Microsoft Teams, Slack, or SharePoint.

Mobile: Read articles on the fly

Mobile: Quickly publish intelligence from the field

TECHNOLOGY CASE: How Netflix uses machine learning to guide users to the most relevant content[14]

The Netflix Recommender system is an excellent example of using Machine Learning to sift through large amounts of content in a smart way. Netflix does a great job of providing recommendations based on genre, actors, or directors, which accompanies a "like" system.

One of the reasons Netflix quickly surpassed traditional TV networks is that they use Machine Learning to recommend content viewers may be interested in based on viewing history and other factors. Specifically, Netflix reviews content you watch and offers suggestions based on categories such as actors, genre, and filming location. Over 75% of the programming consumed springs from these recommendations, and the organization estimates its algorithms produce $1 billion a year in value from customer retention.

Personalized content also helps "find an audience even for relatively small niche videos that would not make sense for broadcast TV models because their audiences would be

---

14 David Chong, April 2020, https://towardsdatascience.com/deep-dive-into-netflixs-recommender-system-341806ae3b48.

too small to support significant advertising revenue, or to occupy a broadcast or cable channel time slot."

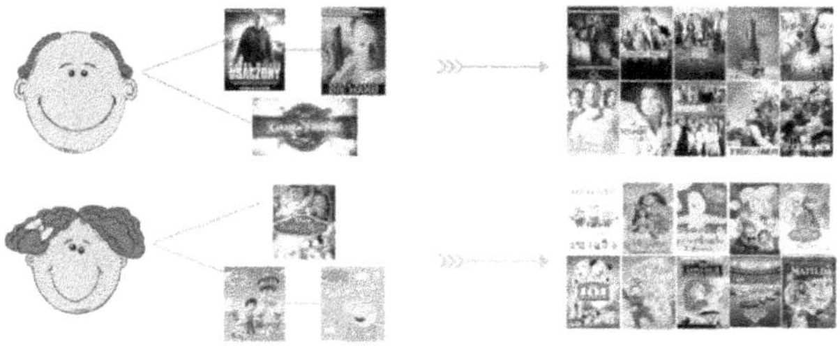

Machine Learning algorithms drive all Netflix recommendations.

For the future, Netflix is already working on new technology intended to improve its recommendation engine. The goal is not only to recommend movies based on what you've seen in the past but also to make suggestions based on what you actually like about your favorite shows and movies.

In 2017, Netflix simplified the feedback function after finding it hard to collect user feedback using the old rating system (based on one to five stars). According to Netflix, ratings increased by 200% with the new binary rating system (thumbs-up or thumbs-down).

TECHNOLOGY CASE: How a global law firm achieved enterprise value from their intelligence platform

Zena Applebaum is a strategy and intelligence professional who is trying to change the legal industry one design thinking workshop at a time. Having pioneered the discipline of Competitive Intelligence in law nearly 20 years ago, Zena shares her passion for the legal and intelligence industries as a speaker and writer. In 2015, Zena was inducted into the Council of CI Fellows. She has been a sessional instructor and a guest lecturer at law schools across North America. Zena is the Director, Market Insights and Proposition Strategy at Thomson Reuters and is based in Toronto, Canada. This is her experience from introducing an Intelligence platform into a global law firm.

The early days of an intelligence career are grounded in finding that one piece of intelligence that will save your organization money or upend the competition. We all look for the silver bullet—the thing that will boost our careers and make us the shining star of the intelligence world. However, even if we could locate such a thing, we would likely not tell anyone other than management and probably leverage it to promote and validate what competitive intelligence (CI) can bring to our organization. It would serve as the catalyst to build out a bigger intelligence unit with more staff and feelings that the CI department has finally arrived.

But the reality is that working as an intelligence professional in a corporate setting rarely, if ever, has that kind of impact. You spend more time answering calls, responding to e-mails, fielding requests for intelligence related to competitor products, or reviewing competitive marketing campaigns to try and read between the lines to ascertain what they truly offer and why. In the practical sense, CI is just reading the news—all the news—local, national, and global, depending on the scope of your role and company. It's reviewing social media sites several times a day, and again, depending on the nature of your organization, this may include Twitter, LinkedIn, Instagram, Facebook, and more. In the real world, CI involves interviewing people—internally and externally—to know what they know and share that across the organization as information is needed. *That* is when transforming information into intelligence. Performing CI in a corporate setting often means collecting data about competitors, their products and marketing, social media, traditional media, trade show visits, and customer or vendor interviews and placing them into some database. For most of us, especially early on in our career or a new role, this means a DIY collection of searchable (we hope!) spreadsheets and documents, maybe a simple web platform if we are technically inclined or, in some cases (although I hope to a lesser degree), well documented, hard-copy folders.

Competitive intelligence has a cool title, and the role's mission is strategic and exciting, but the execution is often a time-consuming grind: especially for solo practitioners with a broad mandate or consultants with many clients. The daily tasks of actually practicing competitive intelligence are not glamourous. For many of us practitioners, that's ok. We know what we are signing up for, and we want to be there. The thrill of the chase makes the "aha!" moments worth it. The more success I found, and the more I uncovered "aha!" moments, the more I realized that like anything, if you can scale the grind, you can deliver more pointed intelligence—while perhaps bringing others who are not skilled CI practitioners into the fold to help as well, whether they realize it or not. **To scale CI, you need technology and a platform to do so**. It's not where most practitioners start, and a CI /MCI platform is not something most companies will fund right away. Yet, once you build up enough success and deliver on enough projects that you have the ear of management, you can start to tell the story of how to be really successful, and the entire company—whether 20 or 20,000 people—will share what they know so your program can evolve from a solo mission to reflect the strength in universal company knowledge.

So, just what is an intelligence platform? And what value does it bring?

First and foremost, an intelligence platform is a technology solution that allows you to scale your CI efforts. Ideally, it automates some or all of your manual labor or menial but necessary tasks, so you are free to review rather than collect data, for example. In an ideal world, a platform would:

1. Aggregate or house internal and external data from multiple databases and surface it all on one view, reducing the need to maintain multiple spreadsheets, searches, and documents. For example, linking a competitor profile (manually curated and maintained) to automated social media feeds to news articles about that same company.

2. Act as a one-stop shop for all secondary research

3. Serve as a platform for information sharing wherein anyone in the organization with knowledge about a competitor or customer can share that information in real-time for anyone else to view, verify (triangulate), and then use as necessary

4. Provide a place to store humint (human intelligence) gathered on a particular topic that can be searched by anyone

5. Increase the speed with which intelligence insights can surface and be worked into strategic plans as the process itself speeds up and is enhanced with a unified taxonomy, search terms, and algorithms.

For most intelligence professionals, the sheer scalability an intelligence platform offers is rewarding and energizing enough. Yet, some great bonus features for a system are worth noting as well. Opening up an intelligence platform to the entire organization—with appropriate security around sensitive data—provides the opportunity for:

- Better customer service
- Strengthened employee engagement and
- Reinforcement of corporate values like collaboration.

This may make an intelligence platform sound a bit like a unicorn, but if used properly, it is truly effective. So let's dig into each additional benefit a bit to explain what we mean.

Better customer service

Whether performing CI in the context of a large global organization like us or employing CI consulting for various customers, clients may assume that anyone from your organization has a basic understanding of who they are, what they do, and why they need CI. If you can, pull together basic information supplemented with an ongoing social media feed and some internal data (ongoing engagements, for example) to have handy when that client reaches out to anyone in the organization—so those beyond the CI team or practitioner who collected the information can see it and know how to respond. A CI platform can act as a CRM system but provide additional insight into the external world. Clients expect that we all know what each other knows, and a CI platform makes that easier to achieve.

Strengthened employee engagement

Most employees want to do a good job and be recognized for the work and value they provide to the organization as a whole. Every employee knows something about the competition—whether in winning or losing direct sales, producing marketing that stands out, or creating a better product. Every employee should think about what he/she/they can contribute to company success, thereby beating the competition. By establishing a CI platform and inviting others to contribute to that effort through logging data, sharing win/loss analyses, and feeding other data into the system and then rewarding that behavior, can convert the entire company into CI hunters and gatherers and encourage employee engagement. Engaged employees who feel like they are part of the mission are statistically more inclined to be happy and effective organization members.

Reinforces collaboration

The employee engagement aspect of the CI platform, if well-executed, can help reinforce corporate values like collaboration, trust, and transparency. If everyone can see what someone else adds to the system and is rewarded for this, they will want to collaborate and share what they know. Reinforcing this idea results in better intelligence gathering and customer service but also enhanced company collaboration.

Added bonus: Visibility

An added bonus is that the CI department—even if it's a department of one—will gain visibility within the organization so that people stop asking, "What do you do? What is competitive intelligence?" as they regularly contribute to the effort and are hopefully observing those contributions turn into real insight for the organization.

Measuring success

In this book, we have presented what seems like the picture of a perfect intelligence platform. It automates collection, allows for two-way communication, encourages employee engagement, and provides everyone in the organization with a view into competitive intelligence. These are the potential benefits, but getting there and fostering buy-in and adoption is not that simple. To truly be successful in creating a platform and encouraging others to use it, you need to consider many things. For example, implementation, design, metrics, and governance considerations must be thought through when you begin the process of choosing and ultimately selecting a platform and vendor. Like any software purchase, you'll need a set of up-front objectives the system should achieve based on your organization's needs. Then, buy or build it accordingly. At the end of this chapter, we provide a non-exhaustive list of some of these considerations, highlighting the things we'd consider in platform implementation.

So, how do you measure success and that elusive ROI?

Before we talk about this, let's first discuss how you can set yourself and your platform up for success: the rollout. Software adoption and use can be difficult as you try to change habits and workflows. You are introducing something brand new, or at the very least, a new way of reading the news, learning about competitors and clients, and evaluating what all of this means. You will want to ensure that if you implement a CI platform and wish to roll it out beyond the CI department, that you do so in a meaningful way with key performance indicators in mind. If no one is actively contributing intelligence information without active solicitation, then making available a platform where people can provide the same is in itself a win—but that is not measurable. **If you can't measure it, it doesn't matter.**

You'll want to provide access and then track engagement activity, looking for things like the number of unsolicited data points we get in a week. A month. A year. How will we maintain engagement? Where can we post the platform link in existing workflows to ensure the best possible results? These are big questions that require time to answer, but management will want to know what they can expect from their investment. Are five new contributions a week enough of a return? Maybe it's ten? Additionally, each data point is not equally weighted, so you will want to employ a mechanism to measure the quantity of data coming in from the outside and the *quality* of that data. If set up well, however, the platform should operate with respect to the data coming in and how those in the organization are using curated data that is now available regularly. This is hard to measure, but you will seek to collect qualitative data—anecdotal evidence of how the platform aids a customer conversation or competitive kick out—alongside how the platform and related content contribute to customer wins from a quantitative perspective (project size and expected revenue). You will want to track requests for new topics added to your monitoring, new pages created in the platform, and the volume of incoming commentary from the field.

After implementing a platform like this for six months, we sent a report to management showing our progress. It read something like:

- 20+ client pages (from four at launch)
- Ten practice/business line pages
- Ongoing requests for more pages/topics to be added
- Reduced e-mail (time savings)
- More time spent on analysis by the team
- One new client identified

The sourcing, testing, and rollout process were so successful that the various departments involved in implementation experienced improved collaboration, developed a better appreciation for each other's deliverables, and improved the working relationship.

After a year, I was able to pull statistics that could tell me, by role, who engaged with the platform and for how long each day. I identified "power users" that I could interview to gather qualitative information on how they were using the system to develop my ROI story for continued investment, as well as gather names of actual customers who were secured partially due to the system's availability and intel that I delivered in an automated fashion (different from the higher-value bespoke work we performed in other areas of the business). Finally, I could point management to when my team saved in automating tasks while still providing high-quality curated intelligence and information, delivering value to the organization.

The ROI of intelligence systems can be difficult to quantify in a meaningful way, so you will want to account for real value (deals won), operational value (time saved, resources freed up), and bonus values around engagement and customer happiness.

Platform panacea

The beginning of this chapter discussed how CI collection could be a grind. We still stand by that, but we are also realists and know that for many CI practitioners on their own in a department or part of a bigger role in research or strategy, that is the reality. It's a DIY spreadsheet and documents folder kind-of situation. But should the opportunity to request or implement a CI platform present itself, I strongly encourage anyone to take it. The platform, which takes some thought and planning to implement (as discussed elsewhere in this book), allows for a scalability of services that will increase the ROI of the entire CI function while also laying the foundation for other benefits such as better collaboration across the organization and, most importantly, stronger customer service.

Whether dealing with internal stakeholders or external customers, there is an assumption that all information is shared equally amongst an organization and that everyone dealing with a customer knows everything that everyone else knows about the stakeholder or customer. Competitive intelligence is at the core of that principle, and we know that that is rarely the case in practice. We tend to know things we have been told or that have been shared with us, but often, that is only part of what we should or could know. Implementing a CI platform and encouraging others in your organization to share what they know brings everyone a step closer to knowing what we all know about CI—it's the holy grail of customer service, organization effectiveness and if harnessed completely, the ultimate competitive advantage.

Checklist to consider for CI Platform Implementation

- Ease of Use (UX/UI)
- Taxonomy
    - Meta tagging and data architecture
    - Unified language across departments and functions within the org
- Data Collection
    - Where are the data sources?

    - Automated data collection—tagging, source master, APIs
- Dashboard Design
- Report Design—Newsletter Templates, etc.
    - Brand management
    - Unification of voice
- Metrics and Analytics
    - ROI
    - "Big Data"—informing collection development, social media presence
    - Legal concerns—privacy
- Governance Plan
    - Governance plan purpose
    - Stakeholders and user groups and roles
    - Bennett Jones Aggregator System roles
    - Sources and content types
    - Permissions
    - Page creation and related responsibilities
    - Service and support
- Training and Adoption

PEOPLE CASE: How Ericsson turned its workforce into Intelligence gatherers

The following is a summary of an article published by Pia Helena Ormerod in CI Magazine.[15]

Ericsson's Competitive Intelligence was built on three pillars:

- The BIC—Business Information Centre—online MCI application
- The EBIN—Ericsson Business Intelligence Network—Intelligence Community for analysis
- The BIAP—Business Intelligence Analysis Program—training program for all EBIN participants

From within Ericsson, a group of just over a hundred analysts were picked. Their area of responsibility was to monitor the marketplace and assess the importance of events, actions, and new technology to Ericsson's competitive strength. For Gabriel Anderbjörk and his team, the task was to transform this group of analysts into a network that was neither project nor line-based. "This was a completely new way to run a team. No one was

[15] Competitive Intelligence Magazine, Vol 5, No. 1, Jan-Feb 2002.

forced to take part, and this increased the powerful group dynamics," Mr. Anderbjörk said. "We turned our analysts into dedicated project, company, and market experts."

It took quite a long time to build up this intelligence network. The first meeting took place in 1997. "It was hard to get people from different markets and divisions to speak to each other, and even harder to get them to share 'their' information with each other. Yet, by breaking the traditional pattern, we achieved a clearer picture of our surrounding world—and that, in turn, was reflected in our BIC," he remarked.

To begin with, the analysts were frightened to share information. "We invited some of them to a seminar in Malaysia and locked ourselves up in a hotel to attack these problems directly—this was just what we needed. We created templates and special forums for their reports, which cut downtime and also helped alleviate any anxiety about writing reports to be read by others," Mr. Anderbjörk shared. By working with templates, all analysts could load their specific information via the intelligence platform, and the person responsible for a special project could easily coordinate all relevant information into a final report, which covered a country, product, or special company. An analysis could be finished within 3-4 weeks.

"Before EBIN, we could spend six months on an in-depth analysis," Mr. Anderbjörk explained. "In the beginning, our role at the center was to act as internal consultants. It was up to us to guide the analysts in how to use the templates. We also told everyone what kind of information we wanted," he recounted. "It is remarkable how much those really close to the market know, but sometimes they do not even realize that they are sitting on extremely valuable information. They just see one piece of the jigsaw."

Mr. Ejdling Martell also found that the analysts inspired each other and became more adept at disseminating information. "And this in turn led to a greater trust from top management," he said.

The BIAP was the third pillar of the program and involved analyst education and training. "We used live cases and worked in project groups of 20-25 people at a time," Mr. Anderbjörk relayed. "The first course took place in 1998, and the participants had to present a report after a couple of months. The analytical competence that was gained clearly impressed top managers, as they were often involved to choose the cases."

"We needed that extra edge BIC[16] provided. We needed it because of increased competition. At the same time, we were inundated with an ever-increasing flow of information, and we needed tools to select the right data quickly. This could only be done via a process run by highly competent people."

Lars Stålberg, Senior Vice President of Corporate Communications, Ericsson

PEOPLE CASE: How an energy company tracks future scenarios

Ulf N Mannervik is co-founder of the global strategy consulting firm NormannPartners, specializing in scenario-based strategy work. He points out that both the power and a key challenge of scenario-based approaches does not exist within scenario analyses per se (even if that must be well-tailored to assess assumptions the business rests upon), but in connecting scenario assessments with ongoing decision-making and follow-up processes in large organizations.

---

[16] BIC—Business Information Center was the corporate intelligence portal at Ericsson.

This requires paying attention to strategy assessment architecture at several time horizons to roadmap designs and embed these as continuous processes and systems. This includes systems for scenario tracking and strategy-progress monitoring to be able to frequently rebalance priorities, initiatives, and sprints—both at the corporate level and relevant functional levels. Building such capabilities is often done effectively over a longer period of time, step-by-step, and always with great attention to the existing DNA and processes of the organization.

A global client in the energy sector developed a scenario-tracking capability. A key success factor was the organization-wide strategy network that was gradually built up around and mobilized for regular assessments of scenario unfolding and strategy implications in different parts of the organization. It helped inform an effective value creation by balancing a mid-term strategy based on the existing oil and gas business with a long-term strategy to build an early leading position in the renewable energy field. The company has since outpaced rivals in both the shift to sustainable energy and in shareholder value.

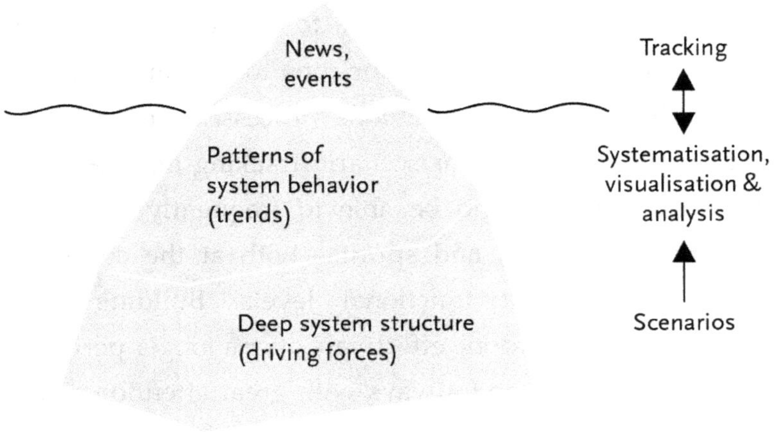

Using MCI to track current events and scenario indicators allows you to dynamically follow how future scenarios are unfolding.

The Future of Intelligence

To any data professional in the business of contributing to the growth of an organization, it is a given that relevant market, industry, and competitive intelligence information is paramount, especially in today's highly disruptive and uncertain future. Seamless collection, analysis, taxonomy, strategy development, and execution are essential, and doing this faster and more accurately than your competitor is a consistent recipe for success.

But many companies are unable to harness the power of data and transform its nature into one that can actually serve the organization. Fundamental questions arise on its strategic importance and the ability to implement and execute on its value given the multitudes of complex interactions, not only between company operations but organizational priorities and communications. This can lead to fragmented and incomplete execution deliverables and moreover, missed windows of opportunities to "strike while the fire is hot" against competitive moves and industry disruptive shifts.

There are certainly shifts in organizational priorities and related culture on customer focus, product development, supply chain management, and other highly susceptible processes under a "perpetual disruptive" microscope associated with the latest pandemic crisis. Given the new 4th Industrial Revolution context (and moreover with the Covid-19 implications), organizations are actually in a constant state of "disruption," whereas only the magnitude of the disruption can vary over time. Now culturally, we are all waiting to return to the "new normal." Unfortunately, no one can tell you what the "new normal" is going to be; (there are as many perspectives in what this definition is comprised of as there are in the number of people giving the perspective!). I have never been comfortable with this "new normal" terminology because it implies some sort of steady-state or constant behavior that should be perceived as being "comfortable and predictable." Viewing sociological and organizational dynamics in that light is myopic and outright dangerous.

The current Covid-19 high-magnitude disruption has certainly affected everyone. But from an organizational sense, there are some companies that have been devastatingly affected, while others seem to "weather the storm" or even prosper under these conditions. And given the nature of disruption as a whole, there is often little to no time of advanced warning as to when, or how bad the magnitude is going to be (remember how the initial reaction to Covid-19 was to simply implement a 2-week "flatten the curve" universal response?).

This is why the content described in this book is critical to any intelligence professional who wants to utilize market forces in the best way to drive business growth. I have worked with Jesper and Gabriel on similar topic presentations, workshops and articles, and their grasp of the knowledge and familiarity with the business challenges are evident. They are uniquely equipped with the talent to outline clearly and articulately the process, external influences and required taxonomy to understand how tools and resources around Artificial Intelligence and Machine Learning can be best utilized to embrace the disruption and develop digital transformational growth from data-driven intelligence.

Therefore, the requirements for the future Intelligence professional need to expand in capabilities, judgements, knowledge, and influence—one that requires a much broader perspective of business and social-economic global implications.

As I see it, there are two main areas of development that are essential to the future strategist:

1. **The new role of the Intelligence Strategist**—An Intelligence Strategist™ has insight into the technology implications and the global, societal, and economic impacts/effects of supply chain

products and services. Someone who is an Intelligence Strategist™ needs to be far more knowledgeable than the traditional CI professional in how all of these elements interconnect to impact business growth.

2. **The development of new IT Tools**—the automation of data analytical tools such as those indicated in this book are essential in managing the onslaught of data amid disruption in real-time: tools utilizing not only AI and ML algorithms that predict certain outcomes based on a multitude of scenario planning landscapes, but ones that can help manage, contextualize and offer prescriptive means on what the data signals offer and how to navigate thru the data and disruption. Competitive Intelligence tools should suggest various plans that will become business growth enablers, rather than simply offering a means to "weather the storm."

Combining these two areas will provide you with intelligence about your competitors, your market landscape, and knowledge that extends beyond the traditional collection of competitive intelligence research. The key to developing successful business growth strategies is integrating relevant competitive data points as an overarching strategy as early as possible. As a result, you get data-based execution plans similar to real-world dynamics.

Organizations will increasingly realize the importance of a near real-time correlation with their markets and that such correlating activities need to be part of every employee's mandate. With today's steadily increasing pace of industry change and information availability, it will be the companies that truly embark on this path for their MCI operations that eventually will be the winners of tomorrow. Organizations that grow their MCI capacity build for the future and will be prepared for the next market disruption before their competitors.

By Paul Santilli

Paul is the manager of Hewlett Packard Enterprise OEM Intelligence and Strategy, and he is the Chair Emeritus of the Board of SCIP (Strategic and Competitive Intelligence Professionals) Association (www.scip.org). Paul resides in Chicago, USA.

Key Takeaways

The following is a summary of the key takeaways from each chapter. Together they offer an executive summary of the main insights of this book.

Chapter 1—Introducing MCI

- The pace of change is accelerating, and there is an overload of information.
- The fear of missing an important piece of the puzzle is growing and can lead to "decision paralysis."
- MCI is about systematically gathering, analyzing, and managing information about your business landscape. It helps drive decisions that improve your competitive advantage.
- MCI fails when it lacks purpose and direction.

Chapter 2—Everything is changing

- MCI must adapt to the new fast-paced, disruptive world.
- The traditional intelligence cycle is obsolete due to decentralized decision-making and non-linear information flows.
- The Intelligence Web is a more suitable way of working in a continuous, non-sequential web or network of

information and analytics exchange, always driven by corporate vision and strategy.

- Without a modern technology platform, efficient and scalable Market and Competitive Intelligence is very difficult, if not impossible.

Chapter 3—Preparing the Grounds

- The six maturity levels of the Garden of Intelligence are:

    1. The Seeds
    2. The Sprouts
    3. The Plants
    4. The Flower Beds
    5. The Shrubberies
    6. The Blooming Garden

- The Information, Technology, People framework is key for managing your Garden of Intelligence.

- The team of gardeners should comprise the following six roles:

    1. Executive Sponsor—Owner of the garden
    2. Director of MCI—Lead gardener
    3. Information specialists—Look after the seeds and plants
    4. Technology specialist—Tends to the equipment and tools
    5. Analysts—Apply fertilizers and water the garden
    6. Decision-makers—Garden produce consumers

Chapter 4—The Six Levels of a "Garden of Intelligence"

- The six different levels and corresponding development phases for your blooming Garden of Intelligence are described and explained in terms of the vision, key matters, ITP and gardeners tasks.

- Each phase requires different focus on the ITP components:

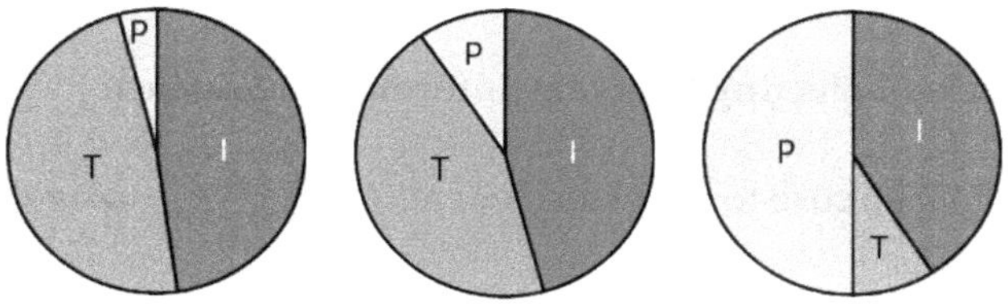

Locating | Planting | Cultivating

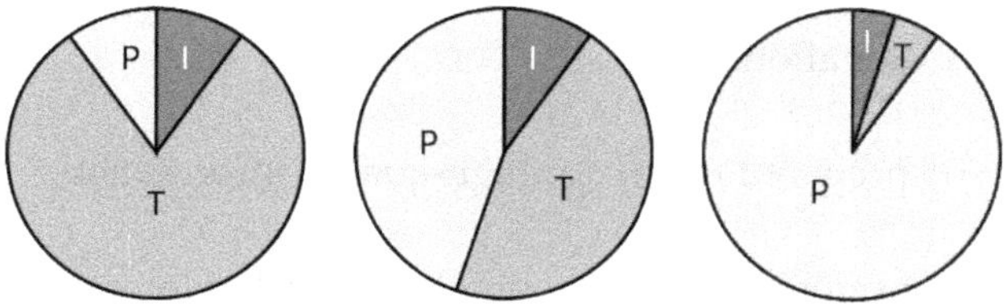

Speading | Burgeoning | Harvesting

- This is the time to reflect on which garden level your organization is right now. What do you need to level up?

Chapter 5—Navigating Information in a Structured Way

- MCI taxonomies are based on business context and decision areas, not content at hand.

- MCI taxonomies are dynamic and adaptable to change.
- MCI taxonomies allow each piece of information to be classified into multiple topics, not just one.
- MCI taxonomies avoid duplicate topics (think in terms of "tags")
- MCI taxonomies are simple and easy to use—for everyone!

Chapter 6—Selecting Relevant Information Sources

- Make sure to build a *mix* of all source types to avoid bias.
- Continuously evaluate your sources to ensure they keep providing both the right quantity and quality of information.
- Be prepared to pay for high-quality information.
- Consider separating content from technology tools to select your sources independently.
- Selecting relevant sources for an enterprise intelligence operation is a complex task, but worth every minute invested in the process.

Chapter 7—How to Build a MCI Technology Platform

- The key purpose of a MCI platform is to provide a single access point to both external and internal sources for all producers and consumers of intelligence within your organization.

- A MCI platform should be much more than simply monitoring web news and producing newsletters detailing past events. In addition to monitoring, MCI platforms should have the capability to support MCI in the discovery and creation of new insights.

- To cope with varied needs and changes over time, an MCI platform must be flexible and easily adapt to new requirements.

- MCI platforms don't work well as stand-alone systems. They must be well embedded and integrated into the organization's eco-system of tools to ensure easy access from the user's preferred platform.

- Find inspiration in the checklist of 14 points to consider when evaluating MCI platforms.

Chapter 8—How to Apply Artificial Intelligence and Machine Learning Technology

- Augmented Intelligence for Market and Competitive Intelligence uses computational algorithms to help place the human end-user in the best position to make informed decisions.

- AI/ML supports, but does not replace, human analysis.

- Ask AI the right question, and you will be greatly rewarded. Ask AI the wrong question, and the opposite holds true.

Chapter 9—How to Create an Intelligence Community of People

- An Intelligent Community is a network of trained knowledge workers who systematically work together to maximize the value of their combined knowledge.
- In an Intelligent Community, members choose whether to participate or not, and the community manager's only recruitment tool is the attraction of the community itself.
- Keep human behavior at heart! A community is built on a combination of trust, altruism, and incentives and must be cultivated and managed accordingly.
- To bypass agoraphobia, we find it helps to provide a steady flow of external information whereby each person can comment and add their opinion or insights—this is the Information Carrier Wave.
- The modus operandi is key to success. Unless entirely transparent and unanimous, community efficiency will suffer significantly and may cause the initiative to fade away.

Chapter 10—How to Prepare People for Change and Disruption

- The future tends to strike by surprise, but MCI boasts tools to mitigate the effects.
- We describe some of the most common foresight tools that can use Market and Competitive Intelligence as a foundation, namely:
  - Scenario planning
  - Business war games

  - Trend radars
  - Early warning systems
  - Innovation management

- Change and disruption can be tremendously costly. For most, the words bear negative connotation: but can instead represent true opportunities for those who are prepared.

- Working models for future preparedness are many. Find those most suitable for your particular organization and culture.

Chapter 11—Becoming a Healthier Organization

- MCI strengthens the competitive advantages of any organization by providing:

  - Healthier Decisions
  - Healthier Market Position
  - Healthier Ways of Working
  - Healthier Financials
  - Healthier Future

- To prove the value of MCI, it must be measured. MCI has concrete and measurable benefits that are universally applicable. They depend on the purpose of MCI. Find those most relevant to your organization.

- Fundamentally, MCI is a decision-support service for the entire organization. It is through these decisions that health will prosper.

What will you do on Monday morning?

While we undertook the final edit of this book in early 2021, the Covid-19 pandemic had hit the world and developed into a huge disruption for many businesses. We saw new MCI trends, tools, and efforts quickly emerge thereafter, many along the lines of the ideas presented in this book. As we stated in the very first section, "With this book, we aim to bring intelligence into the future and the future into intelligence." This seems to be happening even faster than we had originally envisioned.

"Garden of Intelligence" does not end with his book. On the contrary, this only serves as the starting point, joining a newly launched website wherein the authors aim to continue conversations and develop together with you, the reader. The website contains additional material to help grow Gardens of Intelligence, such as blogs, films, presentation, interviews and tools.

Please visit https://www.gardenofintelligence.com to continue your growth!

Let's connect at:

Gabriel Anderbjörk

e-mail: gabriel.anderbjork@gardenofintelligence.com

LinkedIn: https://www.linkedin.com/in/anderbjork/

Jesper Martell

e-mail: jesper.martell@gardenofintelligence.com

LinkedIn: https://www.linkedin.com/in/jespermartell/

Sponsor a Garden

While constructing this book using a garden theme and related terminology, we enjoyed learning more about botanical gardens and plants as part of this process. Since pollination is needed for plants to reproduce, we also learned more about the importance of bees—many plants depend on them or other insects as pollinators. Plants are essential for all life on earth, yet one-fifth of all plant species are threatened by extinction.

Botanic gardens are institutions that hold documented collections of living plants for the purpose of scientific research, conservation, display, and education. Botanic Gardens Conservation International (BGCI) is a plant conservation charity based in Kew, London, England. A portion of the proceeds from this book will be donated to BGCI to help protect gardens and plants all over the world.

BGCI is a membership organization representing botanic gardens in more than 100 countries around the world. Its combined work forms the world's largest plant conservation network, with a mission to mobilize botanic gardens and engage partners in securing plant diversity for the well-being of people and the planet.

Please visit, support, and learn more about their important work at https://www.bgci.org/.

Acknowledgments

Although we stand as the authors of this book, no book is the work of just the author(s). The number of individuals we would like to extend thanks to with regards to the contents of this book is simply far too extensive. And so, collectively, to all customers, partners, competitors, and friends, we would like to offer our sincerest thank you for all of the dialogue, provocative discussions, feedback, and encouragement along the way.

Special thanks to all former colleagues at Ericsson—No one can make a journey like ours without the energy and support you provided all those years ago. And we had so much fun along the way!

Having said this, there are four people who deserve special recognition for the impact they have had on our work:

Anders Thulin, our third team member, our Mr. T (for Technology…). Without his groundbreaking efforts and competence within Artificial Intelligence, Machine Learning, and search technologies, Intelligence2day would not be where it is today.

Lennart Grabe, SVP Corporate Strategy during our time at Ericsson. His belief in, and support of, all new ideas we suggested to bring Ericsson's competitiveness to new heights made it possible to prove our approach to MCI. Lennart has also worked alongside us at Comintelli as a board member from the very start. Without him, we would most likely not be doing what we are today.

Ben Gilad, our mentor during our later years at Ericsson. As a member of Comintelli's first Board of Directors and a long-time friend, Ben has inspired, provoked, criticized, and energized us, constantly keeping us on our toes and steering us down the right path.

Christian Bjersér, our long-term colleague and friend, both at Ericsson and Comintelli. His sarcastic wit and cold sharpness used to challenge many of our thoughts is unparalleled. He has served as a source of frustration, fun, and innovative thinking that has driven us to level up.

Finally, for those who directly helped out with this book, thank you to:

- **Ben Gilad** for his skeptical yet humorous foreword
- **Paul Santilli** for an urgent yet optimistic afterword and contributions on AI and Machine Learning
- **Sven Hamrefors** for his research-based and very insightful advice on the structure and focus during our final editing work

- **Håkan Edvinsson** for his invaluable lessons and detailed comments in our manuscript on "how to write a book"
- **Ulf Mannervik** for his contribution on scenario indicators in the case section of the book
- **Zena Applebaum** for her contribution on enterprise value in the case section of the book
- **Torbjörn Johansson** for his pedagogical illustrations that helped us visualize our complex thoughts

Finally, we would like to take this opportunity to thank all colleagues at Comintelli, past and present. When Anders, Gabriel and Jesper started out in 1999, it was from very humble beginnings; it is remarkable how many amazing people have gotten onboard to join the journey. Thank you so much for believing in the organization and for all the hard and rewarding work! This book is a direct result of all the inspiration and education we have experienced together.

We are truly grateful and hope to have planted some seeds of intelligence with you along the way.

Glossary of MCI Terminology

A

Analysis. Analysis involves examining complex information to ascertain what has happened (or is about to happen), what it means and what should be done about it. The fundamental forms of analysis are: deduction, induction, pattern recognition, and trend analysis.

Application Programming Interface (API). An interface that provides programmatic access to service functionality and data within an application or database. Companies use APIs to serve the needs of building an ecosystem of applications.

Artificial Intelligence (AI). Artificial intelligence (AI) applies advanced analysis and logic-based techniques, including Machine Learning, to interpret events, support and automate decisions.

Automatic Indexing. Automatic indexing uses a program to select words or phrases to identify content. It often employs several indexing languages (such as a classification scheme, natural language, a controlled vocabulary, a standard industry code, or a country code).

B

Boolean Logic. Boolean logic refers to an algebraic system in which all values are reduced to TRUE or FALSE (that is, 1 or 0 in the binary system), and thus forms the basis for all electronic computing. In the context of information retrieval, Boolean operators may be used for manipulating search terms or to represent relationships between entities. The operators most frequently used are: AND (the logical product), OR (the logical sum), and NOT (the logical difference). The AND operator is used to retrieve documents that contain all the chosen search terms, no matter where they appear in the document. Increasing the number of terms helps to narrow the search. The OR operator will retrieve documents that contain at least one of the search terms. The use of additional terms will broaden the search. The NOT operator is used to exclude from the results any documents which contain the specified term or terms; thus narrowing the search. Search results may be graphically represented by using a Venn diagram. The terms are derived from the British mathematician George Boole (1815-1864), who devised the original system.

Business Environment. A Business environment encompasses all those factors that affect an organization's operations, including customers, competitors, suppliers, distributors, industry trends, substitutes, regulations, and government developments. It may also be referred to as an operating environment.

Business Intelligence (BI). Business Intelligence is concerned with information technology solutions for transforming the output from large data collections into intelligence; usually through the integration of sales, marketing, servicing, and support operations. It covers such activities as customer relationship management, enterprise resource planning, and eCommerce using data mining techniques. Those people involved in business intelligence tend to regard it as one aspect of Knowledge Management. Systems based on business intelligence software were formerly known as Executive enterprise reporting, Intelligence Analysis, Market Intelligence, Strategic early warning, and Technological Intelligence.

C

Cloud Computing. Cloud computing is a style of computing in which scalable and elastic IT-enabled capabilities are delivered as a service using Internet technologies.

Communication. Communication is the process whereby knowledge is codified into information by the transmitter, passed through a medium to a receiver, who then reconverts that information into new knowledge.

Community of Practice (CoP). A Community of Practice is an informal, self-organizing, interactive group that develops in response to a specific, work-related activity, subject, practice, or problem of mutual interest. Membership is determined by participation and may transcend hierarchical and organizational boundaries. It provides a means for developing best practices or solutions to problems through communication, that is, through participation in exchanging information and creating knowledge. A community of practice may use a variety of media for this purpose, including face-to-face meetings, reports, e-mail, instant messaging, collaborative workspaces, and intranets. Communities of practice can sometimes make a major contribution to social capital in organizations. A CoP may sometimes be called a Community of purpose or commitment, and a large, geographically dispersed community is often referred to as a Network of practice.

Competitive Intelligence (CI). Competitive Intelligence is a systematic and ethical program for gathering, analyzing, and managing any combination of data, information, and knowledge concerning the business environment in which an organization operates: that, when acted upon, will confer a significant competitive advantage or enable sound decisions to be made. Its primary role is strategic early warning.

Competitive Monitoring. Competitive monitoring is intended to gain early warning through regular, frequent, and proactive monitoring and reporting of changes and trends in your business environment. These changes may stimulate more intensive research or call for the use of more sophisticated analytical techniques. When confined to competitors, it is known as Competitor activity tracking.

Competitor. A competitor is any organization that offers the same, a similar, or a substitute product or service in the field of endeavor in which an organization operates.

Corporate Security. Corporate security aims at protecting knowledge assets, whether in the form of physical entities or intellectual (tangible and intangible) property.

Crawler. A crawler uses existing Internet search engines to carry out automatic search and retrieval of selected information on behalf of a user. It may also be known as a web crawler.

Current Awareness Service. A current awareness service makes available knowledge of what is being done in specific fields of endeavor through documents (such as notes, abstracts, e-mail clippings, selective dissemination of information and database records) or orally (such as face-to-face or telephone conversations).

D

Dashboard. A dashboard is a visualization tool that provides graphical depictions of current key performance indicators to enable faster response to changes in areas such as sales, customer relations, performance assessments, and inventory levels.

Data. Data consists of unconnected facts, numbers, names, codes, symbols, dates, measurements, observations, words and other items of that nature that are out of context, and that only acquire meaning through association.

Database. A database is a collection of interrelated data stored together without harmful or unnecessary redundancy and structured in such a manner as to serve one or more applications. The data is stored so that they are independent of programs that use the data.

Document. A document contains recorded human knowledge, in any format: or is information structured in such a way as to facilitate human comprehension. Essential elements usually include the identity of the originator(s), one or more addresses, a title, the date of origin, relevant information and where feasible, one or more signatories.

E

Enterprise Content Management. Enterprise content management refers to the use of appropriate technology, software, and methods to create, collect, manage, store, retrieve and disseminate content of any kind, including documents and unstructured information, within an organization to better achieve the aims and goals of the enterprise. The practice is sometimes inappropriately referred to as Enterprise Search.

Explicit Knowledge. Explicit knowledge consists of anything that can be codified, or expressed in words, numbers, and other symbols (such as plans, marketing surveys, customer lists, specifications, manuals, instructions for assembling components, scientific formulae, graphics) and can, therefore, be easily articulated, usually in the form of documents, processes, procedures, products and practices.

Extensible Mark-Up Language (XML). Extensible mark-up language allows content producers to add metadata to non-text items, such as image, audio, or video files, and facilitates retrieval of unstructured information (an important aspect of Knowledge Management).

H

Humint. Humint is an abbreviation for human intelligence that is gathered by people directly from people, rather than from published sources, hence so-called Soft information. It may be conducted face-to-face, by means of telephone or facsimile or online (e-mail, chat rooms, intranets, etc.).

Hypertext Markup Language (HTML). Hypertext markup language is the coding language for creating hypertext documents for use on the World Wide Web. It is like a typesetting code, where blocks of text are surrounded by codes that indicate how it should appear. In addition, HTML allows one to specify a block of text or word that is linked to another file on the Internet.

I

Indexing. Indexing provides a means of labeling documents using freely selected keywords or phrases (natural language) or authorized descriptors from a taxonomy or thesaurus (controlled vocabulary), or any combination of those, together with some means of indicating its location in the system.

Information. Information consists of data arranged in some sort of order (for instance, by classification or rational presentation) so that they acquire meaning or reveal associations between data items. Information may also be defined as a physical surrogate of knowledge (language, for instance) used for communication.

Information Management. Information management is the means by which an organization maximizes the efficiency with which it plans, collects, organizes, uses, controls, stores, disseminates, and disposes of its information, and through which it ensures that the value of that information is identified and exploited to the maximum extent possible. The aim has often been described as getting the right information to the right person, in the right format and medium, at the right time. It is sometimes referred to as: Enterprise information management, Information resources management, or Business Intelligence, especially in connection with relevant software.

Information Overload. Information overload refers to the existence of, and ease of access to, bewildering amounts of information, more than can be effectively absorbed or processed by an individual. It often results in an obsessive addiction to new information in an attempt to clarify matters. This may induce a continual state of distraction, which leads to loss of productivity and interrupts social activities. It is also known as Information Fatigue Syndrome and, more colloquially, as Infoglut or Datasmog.

Information Retrieval. Information retrieval involves the identification, location, and collection of specific documents, information contained within those documents or metadata describing those documents from any suitable source.

Information System. Information system refers to the application and software that perform business functions or support key processes. Performance criteria concern the software's quality and functionality, flexibility, and speed and cost of development and maintenance.

Intellectual Capital. Intellectual capital refers to the total knowledge within an organization that may be converted into value or to produce a higher value asset. The term embodies the knowledge and expertise of employees, brands, customer information and relationships, contracts, internal processes, methods and technologies and intellectual property. It equates, very approximately, the difference between the book value and the market value of an organization. Intellectual capital is also referred to as intellectual assets, intangible assets or invisible assets.

Intelligence. Intelligence is high-level, processed, exploitable information.

Intelligence Audit. An Intelligence audit is an examination of an organization's current level of intelligence activities with the objective of improving those operations to gain, and maintain, a significant competitive advantage. It involves:

- identifying those people engaged in intelligence or related operations, together with their levels of expertise
- locating collections of information, as well as other relevant resources, concerning the organization's business environment
- establishing a set of key intelligence topics or ascertaining management intelligence needs

Intelligence Agents. Intelligent agents are software programs that are capable of assisting their users by performing predefined tasks on their behalf. They may, for example, automatically, and simultaneously, monitor a number of websites to identify, filter and collect relevant information: and subsequently recognize patterns or other significant combinations of information; report the results to the user; and offer suggestions to solve a specific problem, draw inferences, or determine appropriate actions.

Invisible Web. Invisible web is the portion (estimated to be between 60 and 80 percent) of total web content that consists of material that is not accessible by standard search engines. It is usually to be found embedded within secure sites, or consists of archived material. However, much of the information may be accessed through a library gateway, a Vortal, or a fee-based database service.

K

Key Intelligence Topics (KITs). Key intelligence topics are those topics identified as being of greatest significance to an organization's senior executives and which provide purpose and direction for Competitive Intelligence operations. Key intelligence topics are invariably derived from a series of interviews. They are then grouped into appropriate categories and allocated a priority, usually by the same or a representative group of people. The basic categories are:

- strategic decisions and actions (including the development of strategic plans and strategies)
- early-warning topics (for example, competitor initiatives, new technology developments, and government actions)

- descriptions of key players (including competitors, suppliers, regulators, and potential partners)

Knowledge. Knowledge is a blend of experience, values, information in context, and insight that forms a basis for building new experiences and information or achieving specific goals. It refers to the process of comprehending, comparing, judging, remembering, and reasoning. Knowledge is data that has been organized (by classification and rational presentation), synthesized (by selection, analysis, interpretation, adaptation, or compression), made useful (by presenting arguments, matching needs and problems, assessing advantages and disadvantages) and acted upon. Knowledge is the uniquely human capability of interpreting and extracting meaning from information. It may be thought of as a structured (inter-related) set of concepts in the mind.

Knowledge Assets. Knowledge assets are bodies of knowledge that are of value to an organization, including previously unarticulated expertise and experience held by individuals. They may take the form of documents, databases, individuals or groups of people, and include records of projects or activities, knowledge maps, links to networks or communities of practice, reports, standard operating procedures, patent specifications, licenses, copyright material, taxonomies, glossaries of terms, and so on. Knowledge assets are sometimes referred to as Corporate intellectual assets, or Corporate memory.

Knowledge Management (KM). Knowledge Management is an integrated, systematic process for identifying, collecting, storing, retrieving, and transforming information and knowledge assets into knowledge that is readily accessible to improve the organization's performance. The basic tenets of Knowledge Management are to enhance decision-making, foster innovation, build relationships, establish trust, share information and improve learning. The means for doing so might include apprenticeship schemes and mentoring programs, briefings and debriefings, bulletin boards, databases, documents, educational and training programs, knowledge maps, meetings, networks, and visits. Performance improvements may be affected through enhanced learning, problem-solving, strategic planning, and decision-making.

Knowledge Management System. Knowledge Management System is a process and procedure for enabling Knowledge Management. It usually incorporates a search engine, data-mining facilities and—since knowledge is primarily embodied in people—an expertise directory or location service (known as a Knowledge map). Content may include profiles of key people, industry trends, market surveys, descriptions of current and proposed projects or activities, solutions to past problems, and discussion group facilities. The term also implies the creation of a culture and information structure that promotes information sharing and innovation and places considerable emphasis on learning and personal development.

Knowledge Map. A Knowledge map may be either or a combination of both of the following:

- a graphical display (either hierarchical or in the form of a Semantic network) of the core Knowledge, together with the relationships between various aspects of a subject or discipline

- a Directory (incorporating identity, location, and subject expertise) of people possessing, or having access to, specific knowledge or experience

In the latter sense, it is a guide to, not a repository of, knowledge or expertise. A critical element is that those people whose details are incorporated must be traceable through keywords describing their area of expertise or subject knowledge. Sometimes referred to as an Expertise database or Expertise location service, it is often compiled with the aid of Expertise locator software. When properly compiled and maintained, it may be by far the most valuable of all Knowledge Management tools. It is often referred to by its more popular term: Yellow pages.

M

Market Intelligence (MI). Market Intelligence concerns the attitudes, opinions, behavior, and needs of individuals and organizations within the context of their economic, environmental, social, and everyday activities. The emphasis is on consumers—product, price, place, promotion.

Market and Competitive Intelligence (MCI). MCI is about systematically gathering, analyzing, and managing information about your business landscape. It helps drive decisions that improve your competitive advantage.

Marketing Research. Marketing research is the study of methods of selling and promoting a product or service, or gathering information that will support a marketing campaign (such as qualitative and quantitative data concerning customer preferences and behavior).

Metadata. Metadata is information (in the form of a metatag) that describes an Internet document and facilitates its retrieval. It is very similar to a bibliographic reference, but—where present—is often more extensive, and may include author, title, affiliation, sponsor, abstract, keywords, language, publisher, date published, contact details, classification scheme, and so on: the most useful probably being keywords.

O

Open Source Information. Open source information is unclassified published information. It includes non-proprietary grey literature as well as information published electronically (on the Internet, for example).

P

Portal. Portal is a website that acts as a gateway to the Internet by providing a broad and diverse range of services, including directories, search engines, links, e-mail, reference tools, forums or chat facilities, access to online shopping and banking, games, entertainment and more.

S

Search Engines. Search engines are microprocessor-driven software programs capable of successfully retrieving information from computer networks or databases to match the needs of searchers. They automatically index keywords in context, usually by using robots, and then search those indexes for keywords that match the user's request. Generally speaking, they are more suitable than directories for conducting research. Current developments may incorporate visualization techniques.

Semantic Networks. Semantic networks represent knowledge in the form of concepts (known as nodes) and links (that indicate the relationships between concepts). A concept is an abstract class or set consisting of items or things that share common features or properties.

Server. Server is a computer, or software package, that provides a specific service to client software running on other computers. A single server machine may have several different server packages, thus providing many different services to clients on the network.

Social Media. Social media is a combination of sociology and information technology that allows people to publish their own content and to establish business or personal relationships.

Software as a Service (SaaS). Software that is owned, delivered, and managed remotely. The provider delivers software based on one set of common code and data definitions that is consumed in a one-to-many model by all contracted customers at any time on a pay-for-use basis or as a subscription-based on use metrics.

Strategy. Strategy is the timely adoption of courses of action and the allocation of resources necessary for carrying out the basic long-term goals and objectives of an enterprise, emphasizing achieving something different or unique. Strategy is the calculation and coordination of ways and means to achieve ends. An organization's strategy may be represented visually by a strategy map, which is a powerful communication tool. Strategy formulation involves the right brain, calling for creativity, and the ability to deal with large volumes of information and visualize a broad perspective.

SWOT Analysis. A SWOT analysis is the evaluation of available information concerning the business environment to identify internal strengths and weaknesses, and external threats and opportunities. SWOT analysis is also known as Situational analysis and, when applied to competitors, as Competitor profiling.

T

Tacit Knowledge. Tacit knowledge is the product of interaction between people or between people and their environment. It refers to knowledge that is gained only experientially and, therefore, cannot be readily articulated or explained to inexperienced parties (for example, drawing, painting, writing, tying a knot, planning, decision-making). An individual will acquire tacit knowledge only by gathering information, relating it to existing knowledge, and accumulating experience; it involves judgment, intuition, and common sense. In groups, tacit knowledge exists in the practices and relationships that develop through working together over time. The major challenges are in its recognition, sharing, and management.

Taxonomy. A taxonomy, in its original form, refers to the science of the classification of living and extinct organisms. In modern parlance, it applies to any system or software designed to organize information or knowledge so that it may be more easily stored, maintained, and retrieved. It usually reflects the language and culture of a specific enterprise or industry and acts as the authority for identifying documents and the content of knowledge maps. A taxonomy is often created by reference to several thesauruses, classification schemes, or indexes using a combination of human intellectual effort and specialized software. A taxonomy offers a means of classifying documents and other items of information into hierarchical groups to make them easier to identify, locate and retrieve. It consists of a structure (or thesaurus), which embodies the terms and their relationships, and a set of applications, which provide the means to identify and locate the information.

Topic Maps. Topic maps are designed to facilitate the organization and navigation of large information collections through the use of an open (non-controlled) vocabulary using topics, associations, and occurrences. A topic may represent any concept, including subject, person, place, organization, and event. Associations represent the relationships between those concepts; and occurrences represent relevant information resources. Although sometimes used when referring to an ontology, taxonomy, or thesaurus, it may, in fact, incorporate any combination of these.

U

Unstructured information. Unstructured information refers to the content of any document that has no defined or standard structure to allow for its convenient storage and retrieval. Examples include blogs, e-mails, images, audio and video files, and wikis.

Index

www.ingramcontent.com/pod-product-compliance
Lightning Source LLC
Chambersburg PA
CBHW071232050326
40690CB00011B/2081
9781634629331